To Tony

Poetic Reflections

Edited by Bobby Tobolik

anchorbooks

Poetry by the People
for the People

anchorbooks

First published in Great Britain in 2005 by:
Anchor Books
Remus House
Coltsfoot Drive
Peterborough
PE2 9JX
Telephone: 01733 898102
Website: www.forwardpress.co.uk

© Copyright Contributors 2005

SB ISBN 1 84418 410 2

Foreword

Anchor Books is a small press, established in 1992, with the aim of promoting readable poetry to as wide an audience as possible.

We hope to establish an outlet for writers of poetry who may have struggled to see their work in print.

The poems presented here have been selected from many entries, and as always editing proved to be a difficult task.

I trust this selection will delight and please the authors and all those who enjoy reading poetry.

Bobby Tobolik

Editor

Contents

The Poems

My Mum

My mum was born in Liverpool
But grew up in Coventry.
Times were hard with Mrs Smith,
So kind but yet so wee.

My mum was a Modette
And longed for a Vespa scooter.
To me they sound like a hairdryer,
With a pathetic, dinky hooter.

My mum joined the Wrens
And trained to be a dental nurse.
Back in the days when she had pence
For a night out in her purse.

My mum left the Wrens
And salty seadogs to have me,
A massive sacrifice, but a happy one,
Then along came another three.

My mum no longer works,
Due to her lung disease,
But over the years she's gained new skills
And obtained employment with ease.

My mum is forgiving,
With a desire for unconditional love.
She's been pushed to the limit
By her sons, but not by Him above.

My mum quit smoking, passed her driving test,
But the love she gives us all In all
Is what she does the best.

I Dunne

April Fool

A man on the phone intones in slow
And measured voice
'This is PC Jones. I've news about
Your wife. She's had
A mishap.' Then the line goes dead.
I pause in shock.
I ring our home, but no reply.
I try police.
Their records note no thing amiss
With cherished spouse.
I ache for man to call again;
To no avail.
I head for home with thoughts now numb,
Besieged by fears.
Relief exceeds all bounds when there
She stands alive
And well. Although it's April 1st,
It's not a joke.
The swine requires a brain transplant.
Perhaps he lacks
That sense one's loved, which people need
To feel alive.
Perhaps corroding hate consumes
His sadist mind.
I faintly feel a tiny grain
Of pity calm
The fury burning out of hand
Within my soul.
May God forgive his hellish hoax
That drained my heart.

Henry Disney

April Fool

Who is the April fool
I am for fooling it
How many
Times have I been caught out
Not anymore
I will make a point
Of staying in bed
Till way after 12 o'clock

E Bevans

Seamus And His Mouse

My cousin's cat is Seamus, in Warwick is his home,
The castle grounds are close at hand, where Seamus likes to roam.
He'll catch a mouse and bring it in,
Unharmed, to show his mum.
She doesn't much appreciate
The gift of such a plum.
One day young Seamus loosed his mouse
Upon the dark hall floor,
Retired upstairs upon the bed
And thought of Mouse no more.
Two hours his mum was chasing it;
Despairing, called him down.
He came, she says, reluctantly,
As if a cat could frown!
Under the dining table he sat
And watched his mum at chase.
Then panicked Mouse; near human was
By far the deadlier place!
Between the soft front paws he ran,
A sanctuary was that!
Then turned and looked out at Mum
Between the front paws of the cat!
And Seamus looked, and sniffed a bit,
And more than ever bored,
Got up and sauntered back to bed,
While round the skirting board
His mum and Mouse resumed their chase, till safely caught at last,
To garden's end was Mouse restored, all fears of Seamus past!

Kathleen M Hatton

April Fool's Day

The 1st April is April Fool's Day
Before 12 noon lots of games we can play
The children love it as we did once
At school they play tricks - whether dux or dunce

Adults take part sometimes too
And when I once worked in a shop I knew
That things were getting out of hand
When the manager sent me for a 'long stand'.

I searched for ages but couldn't find
Just what the manager had in mind
'Ha, ha, April Fool,' said he
As I stood and had a cup of tea.

Sheona M Campbell

Tip Tip Hooray

Today is Saturday and the time is nine, switch on the telly for the
morning line.
As the picture appears on screen, the Channel 4 team can be seen.
First there's big Mac, waiting to tell you which horses you should back.
Good old Mac, always there to make a wisecrack.
Then there's Tanya Stevenson, you can back her tips at evens or
odds on.
She can tell you which horse is a force when running at its
favourite course,
Which horse has a late burst, and may cross the line first,
Or could instead, get caught and beaten by a short head.
So to Jim McGrath, always good for a laugh,
To Jim time form is the best, so forget the rest.
Next we see Leslie Graham, her husband's a trainer,
And knows how to get a horse in the frame.
Then it's on to Tommo, what a tout, knows racing inside out,
He's no beginner, been known to tip many a winner.
So to Graeme Goode, calls the runners as they race,
Tells you whose leading or setting the pace.
As the race nears the end, perhaps they're on the final bend,
If there were eighteen runners or more, his throat could well be sore.
Now it's the turn of John Francome, and Mike Cattermole,
They have an equally important role, to portray and tip a winner today.
Bookmakers as the name suggests, encourage you to lay your bets,
A market they do make, offering odds that you would like to stake,
So all of your money they can take.
Like the scoop six, you have to be in it to win it,
But like we're told, racing's a funny old game, innit?
To those of you I didn't mention, it was without intention,
So please don't feel rotten because I have forgotten
The names of some who presented the morning line,
Saturdays at nine.

David Parker

Untitled

Love will strike
When you least expect
Often for the mess you've left

Christopher Bolton

On Laughter

I had an inspiration once,
but after I got an ointment
from the chemist,
it soon cleared up.

Hans Denndorf

Catch Bookworming Willie

(A bookseller's lament)

Oh someone catch Bookworming Willie
Who always reads my book so silly.
His unwashed, stained fingers damage all my bookshop ware,
His reading's carefree and never fair!

After Willie has it all read,
My new-ordered stock is almost dead!
I'll sell not a single dog-earred book,
That his filthy hands have cruelly took.

Secretly crossing out a line
That sounds nae fine
Though this property
Is surely mine.

Go, go, go, Willie,
To a library,
And spare and spotless
My next delivery!

S Wilson

Under His Head

A simple man, named Joe McFred,
Slept with his money under his head,
Burglars will know,
Where your head is Joe,
I sleep the other way round, he said!

Joan M Wylde

The Naughty Puppy

(At a Christmas party)

Oh, it was an awful to-do
No one could open the door
The puppy was rushing around the floor
Tearing paper and scratching away.
At last, with a crash and a bang
The door swung open to reveal
That bad pup and the puddle on the floor.
Small wonder we couldn't get into the loo!
Oh, it was an awful to-do!

Blanche C Rice

The Comfort Of Books

In the vaulted library the smell of the past
Takes us away from the noisy world, away from the blast.

The occasional pin-fall, the occasional snore,
Does not mean that the past is a bore.

The comfortable book-world, cosy and warm,
Means a world of progress, away from the harm.

Managers should sleep here to put their feet on the ground,
To balance their lofty ideas away from dollar and pound.

Maybe that's it, the mightiest executive's ultimate promotion,
Stamp collecting, cataloguing and lengthy devotion.

Alan Bruce Thompson

Trust Again

(Dedicated to Dave Rothwell from Garry. Dated 16/10/04)

A man I can trust again
He has helped to ease my pain
To let me share his cherished treasure
From him to me this is so rare

The treasure you see is his wife
This may have well saved my life
His wife is named Claire
The two together have showed me so much care

So from me to you
All I want to say is thank you
For you both I will pray
God bless you Dave, this I must finally say.

Garry Bedford

What Shape Are Your Golden Balls?

I booked my flight to Lisbon to cheer our lads' first game
I thought they would play their hearts out, but it really was quite tame
Then Lampard scored a goal for us, and we held them back with ease
We then eased off the pressure, thinking they were on their knees

But those Frenchmen, they came back at us, although we thought
we'd win
Then who do you think it was that scored? Zidane, like a rocket the
ball went in
And then he had a penalty, what a terrific shot
Points that we had in the bag, he grabbed the blooming lot

What were we doing, are the Beckham Boys fit?
If they don't play better than this, they can pack their kit
It's now Thursday night, we are off again, we must win this one
for sure
Someone said the Swiss would be easy, there are no easy teams
any more

Now we are here, it's Thursday, it's the Swiss we need to beat
This is the time our players need to turn up all the heat
They did it well; it was Rooney's turn, two goals, what a player
There was more to come, Gerrard's the name, the third goal was
the slayer

It's Monday night, all should be fit and rested, and full of steam
You need to win Croatia, no messing about, full of flight, fulfill
that dream
So Mr Beckham do your stuff, and show us how to play
We need three goals, but don't stop at that, make sure you're
through today

The Croats came out full of hope and were heading for our net
Within the first few minutes they had scored, it wasn't hard to get
That made our team very nervous, and they struggled on to win
It was our old friend Mr Scholes who eventually popped one in

Then came our young genius, Rooney is his name
A bit of fancy footwork, then two more goals to claim
The game had still more goals to come, the Croats scored once more
And then some fancy football, Lampard scored and almost closed
                                                                    the door

Our next is against Portugal, the host team of the cup
Good luck to all our players, we must keep this standard up

L Woodhead

Leicester V Everton

I just blew in from windy city
As did Doris Day
Thought first half we played well
Second half - gave goal away

You expect to lick the *toffee* men
But that's not how it went
Though we were saved from *sticky* end
Thanks to Marcus Bent

Expect no *'Mersey'* next Saturday
But Liverpool aren't at their prime
Yes lads, you can do it
By giving their *Gerr-ard* time

Bernie Adams

You've Been There

(This poem means a lot to me, as three years ago I lost my mum to cancer, and so it was read at her funeral. She also saw and kept the poem when I wrote it for her)

You've been there through the good times
and all the sad times too.
There can never be a person
who understands like you.
You take care of my worries
and thoughts that don't belong.
How can somebody be so soft,
and yet be very strong?
To put up with the things you have,
and do the things you've done.
There could never be a person
who is dearer than my *mum*.

Lynne Farley

Your Secrets Are Safe With Us

I have ten porcelain dolls
Who are my pride and joy
Nine of them are beautiful ladies
And the tenth a handsome boy

They all wear gorgeous outfits
And always have a smile on their face
They really look quite splendid
With never a hair out of place

All the dolls live in my lounge
Each of them has a name
They all are very attentive
And none of them ever complain

They listen to my moans and groans
My ups and downs as well
I love confiding in my dolls
Because I know they will not tell

When people ask do I wish the dolls could talk
I say, 'Oh no, no, no'
That would not be a good idea at all
I much prefer the status quo

Jackie Richardson

Untitled

There was an old man from the west
Who slept with his boots on his chest
They did keep him warm
But for this he was scorned
So he bought a small blanket instead

Thomas Latcham

Californian Babe On My Mind

Golden-haired babe
With LA smile
Brown-eyed angel
Shimmering in the Californian sun
Sexy legs and ruby-red lips
You left me breathless
Addicted to your love

In the Mojave Desert
We sealed our vows
Kissed and snuggled
The whole night through
Hand in hand
Heart to heart
We savoured the taste
Of midnight love

Pacific blue
Warm waters divine
Blended our hearts
As we tasted sweet wine
Hispanic welcome
Te amor my bride

Frisco sounds
Clasp in your hair
We dined on Mexican
Castanets filled the air
Promises fulfilled
Designed for two
Californian babe
I love you true

Peter Paton

Valentine's Day

Valentine's Day is a special day in the year
When we send a card to someone we love and hold very dear
In days gone by the card was signed 'from an admirer' you see
But these days it's no secret and signed for all to see.

The words are so special and the meanings too
Sometimes words fetch tears between you and me
Love is shared by two people you see
And will go on forever till eternity.

I married my valentine on D-Day - June 6th 1953
In Coronation week I became Mrs Ridley
Paul, Helen and Mark complete our family
So thank you my valentine for choosing me.

Marjorie Ridley

On Reflection: A Valentine Warning

It was a lovely morn full of promise and sun; Narcissus felt the day
would be a lucky one.
He opened his bedroom window wide, looked longingly to the lake,
contentedly sighed;
For crystal clear water the sun does make, the boy was drawn to his
image like a duck to a drake:
'Oh, Mirror, Mirror, you lovely water, someone's going to have
a *damned* lucky daughter.'

With (self) love in his step he pirouetted down the stairs, stepped
outside naked (when you're gorgeous, who cares!)
He took his morning bath in summer dew; he growled with pleasure
like a dog with a chew.
He puffed and polished, primped and preened; he was nothing if not
grossly over-weened.
'Gentle Breeze who suckles at my cheeks, you'll feast on this truffle
for many a week.'

Narcissus trotted urgently (such the desire to kiss his reflection), he
passed young Echo who glowed mightily lest she get the
boy's attention,
'Hello, Narcissus,' the girl breathlessly said; but he pushed past sweet
Echo cooing sonnets to himself instead.
At last he reached the pool, flushed from his rampant heart; gazed
adoringly into the lake, watched his lips temptingly part:
'Oh, mirrored god on the lake, who's the handsomest man that God
did make?'

There Narcissus lapped greedily over his Adonis image, for kissing his
reflection fortified body and mind (a bit like spinach!)
This daily ritual complete he sprawled out on a rug, invited the bees to
crawl over him - 'I'm an exotic honey tub!'
He leaned back on a special pillow that wouldn't mess his hair, a
beauty such as his was one he felt he must share:
'Dear Sun above bask my beautiful face, kiss my rosebud mouth,
enjoy
my opulent taste.'

Now 'Mirror, Mirror', that lamented god, turned out to be Echo on
whose heart Narcissus trod;
'You're a silly man with a swollen head; I'll turn you into a
daffy dill instead.
For this *Mirror, Mirror* on the lake doesn't know how much more
of your ego she can take.'
And so Narcissus, that cocky sod, must forever bow over Echo's lake
and deferentially nod!

Carly Dugmore

A Map Of The World

(This poem is dedicated to my husband, Rodger, who not only gave me the map, but the courage and strength to follow the path. Thank you, darling, for being my co-pilot in this ride of a lifetime)

He locked me in irons
And threw out the key.
You broke chains that held me,
Setting me free.

He caged me with cruelty;
Left me to die.
You healed broken wings
And taught me to fly.

He fed me his lies
Till I withered, was doomed.
You nourished my soul
And watched as I bloomed.

He judged me unjustly.
You pardoned the crime.
He put me away.
You served out the time.

He reached out to strike me
His temper unfurled.
He said I'd go nowhere.
You gave me a map of the world.

Ruth Kepthart

Believe

For many years now
I've lived in a prison
Ruled my men
Whose tempers have risen

Been used and abused
Treated like s***
Punched and shouted at
Been kicked and been hit

But I'm still here
Standing with pride
Eyes wide open
Head held high

I've made it through
Survived all the pain
Learnt all the lessons
To love again

Life can be difficult
I have the choice
Listen to myself
Hear my own voice

Believe in my feelings
Believe in myself
Look at me now
Surrounded by wealth

Carol Bosisto

A Joyful Loving Day

(Valentine sonnet for the exquisitely beautiful Ann-maryliss)

So once again the winter days begin
To turn their faces Aprilwards: the sun
At what appears a snail's pace starts his run
Against the night and suddenly we're in
The miserable month, four weeks that give
The elements their one last chance to show
How horrid they can be, to freeze and blow
As well they might, till spring's prerogative
Stuns them to silence. February's weight
Hangs more on older folk each passing year
Yet still retains at least one day to cheer
Their hearts with recollections that vibrate
On tender themes, on loving thoughts that shine
With joy, as mine for thee, sweet Valentine.

Frank Littlewood

Here No More

I close my eyes to say goodnight,
I down some pills to ease my fright,
I feel obliged to live my life,
although this aching can't be right.
I close my eyes and cry some more,
heading down to Heaven's door,
it feels so wrong yet is so right,
the knot is steady, clenching tight.
I plead with God to take my pain,
my soul is Yours, I have no gain,
I know it's wrong but the pain's so true,
what else is there left to do?
Not sure if I will wake again
to see the sun, the moon and rain,
forgive for all that I have done,
my life's a war that can't be won.

Michelle Sims

My Life

Every night I would sit up wondering why,
why am I so shy?
I sit there thinking as time flies by,
sometimes it would even make me cry.
I put on a show for everyone around me,
hoping, wishing that they won't see,
all the pain inside me,
would they want to know,
or would they not,
could they take it, probably not the lot,
could they take knowing that I was used,
or even knowing that I was abused?
I need someone to talk to,
but I don't know who,
who would listen but not judge
who wouldn't have or hold a grudge
I wish the pain would just go away,
just for one day,
so God, all I'm asking of You,
let me live my life and be happy too.

Katie Mason

Confidence

Look down deep
And you will find
You're in there somewhere
You have a strong mind
If only you knew
Just how strong you are
You would fly like a bird
So high and so far
So reach down there deep
And search for your soul
You're longing to be free
To achieve all your goals

Shirley McCabe

Little Baby …

hush little baby don't you cry
I'm in London and not saying bye
even though you make me cry …
I'm still shy and will never lie
even though you do it's not right
believe me baby I don't want to fight
just leave me alone and I will stay
I love you baby, is that OK?

Ig van Niekerk (Jnr)

You're Everything To Me (The Sky, The World And Sea)

You're everything to me; the sky, the world and sea.
When you take me in your arms, I succumb to your loving charms.

There is no world without you; no sky, no world, no sea,
The Earth an empty place, no warmth from the sun would there be.

My heart would break in two, forever, without you,
There'd be no sky, no world or sea, without the love you give so free.

You never cease to amaze me; you're my sky, my world and sea.
Your kisses and love are real, never knew the way I would feel.

Never known such love and emotion, such caring and deep devotion.
You're my sky, my world and sea. You mean everything to me.

Shirley Longford

Little Victories

As I sit in peace reading my book
People ask, 'What are you reading, give us a look?'
They continue to talk, 'Oh, what is it about?'
I tell you what, you read it and then give me a shout.
'I'll wait for the film to come out,' they cry
Please leave me alone and let me get by!
Typical, because of you I have lost my page
My imagination and thought is now but rage
Every day it happens and they never learn
When it's their break, silence my return
I give them respect and they give me none
They talk about the weather, someone give me a gun
Still, being a smoker, I get my own back
Blow it right in their face, a smoky smack
Now I've offended you, without saying a word
Deep joy, revenge, satisfaction all unheard

John Lee

Remembrance

(To Bill)

No thunder clap, no tolling bell,
No silver trumpet sound.
Yet here a shroud of sadness casts
Its shadow all around.

Outside, the many flowers bloom
In regimented rows.
Inside, a long and worthy life
Is drawing to its close.

This room, this bed, with pillowed head,
This wise and weathered face.
This kindly man, a paragon
Of dignity and grace.

He moved his lips as if to speak.
Not him to question why,
But more a silent murmur of
A formal last goodbye.

I watch him slowly slip away,
An old and treasured friend.
Our long and lasting fellowship
Now sadly at an end.

Frank Jensen

I Had You For A Moment

I had you for a moment, a brief but passionate affair
Did you ever feel anything or did you really care
My passion still burns deeply as a candle's golden flame
Oh my sweetest lover, I long for you again

I had you for a moment, I held you in my arms
My love for you enveloped us with all its wondrous charms
But your flame grew dimmer, it's just a flicker now
And I cannot get near you and time will not allow
My heart to yearn forever so I'll let go of you
As I had you for a moment and though you had me too
I had you for a moment
But our time went fast, our passion consumed and destroyed us
We were never meant to last
So my little angel I know that time will tell
That I had you for a moment
And in my heart you will always dwell

Jayne K A Llewin

Curry In Favour

The delivery arrives to an eager eye,
resistance low, anticipation high;
dehydrated from salivating,
I scoop the prize without debating,
messenger left with the price . . . and a door.

A hypnotic odour has deluged my senses,
my rumbling stomach makes no pretences
as, in a trance, I spoon the curry
onto my plate and do not hurry
to stir in the rice with a restrained lore.

So should you enquire what earns my favour,
it would have to be the luscious flavour
of that spicy dish which some pangs sates -
least . . . that is the favourite I ate -
as if you hadn't guessed all that before.

Perry McDaid

Look At Me

Look at me, look at me
Have a good laugh
Yeah, he left me for that eight and a half
So what I'm big
I'm proud of who I am
It just goes to show he couldn't handle me
He wasn't much of a man
Now look at me, look at me
Having a good laugh
Cos your man left you for an eight and a half

Rahela Begum

Fingers And Thumbs

Fingers and Thumbs.
Thumbs and fingers.
All wave together,
Some of them linger.
Small and pudgy,
Full of life,
Eager and cuddly,
Pleading and reaching.
Chubby fingers, little toes,
Nice to nibble, Mummy knows.
Five little fingers, five little toes.

Why are there five? Nobody knows.
Sweet little smile
Just made for me.
I'll give him a hug and
He will gurgle with glee.

Marguerite Gimlinge

Sonnet To Editors

Whatsoever purpose can all this paper have for me?
Should each scrap be destroyed with barely a trace
Remain, might not one learn perhaps to face
Freshly delivered mail. Who would an editor be?
Should this thoughtless rhyme strike some chord,
Or if not, I apologise, seeming sad and contrite.
'Twas written merely in jest, certainly not in spite.
Else I commit hari-kari and fall upon my sword.
Passé, defunct, surely as I scribble arrant nonsense
Possessing not any such sharpened mighty rapier.
In any case, slightly less absurd would it appear
Were such as I to fall upon alleged mightier pens
Should this poem earn scorn, not praise, nor love,
May it be spiked, like its author, as shown above.

Ann Omnibus

I Could Have

I could have been an actress, walking across the stage,
Bowing to my audience in a bygone age,
Speaking, strutting, acting, so beautiful to see,
The stage door Johnnies waiting, to escort only me.

I could have been a ballerina floating gracefully,
Music swelling round me, the people flock to see,
My fans are clapping, I'm in a dream, dancing hours and hours.
Ballet finished, I bow, I smile, accept bouquets of flowers.

I could have been a model, so slim, so tall, so pure,
Wearing clothes made just for me, my future now secure,
The world all mine, men at my feet, a picture to be seen,
Then it happens, talent scout, I'm on the TV screen.

I have been a housewife, mother, I feel quite proud of this,
Cleaning, baking, washing, smiling, it wasn't always bliss,
If I lived my life over, then I would do the same
For destiny is our companion, we walk together down life's lane.

Muriel Rodgers

Ireland

If you follow a rainbow or follow your heart,
You will find a jewel so rare,
With waters that sparkle and meadows of green,
This emerald isle is there.
Smell the musty peat, the shamrock and dew
And feel the heartbeat of the land.
Drink in the air so pure and strong,
Take a fistful of soil in your hand.
Listen to the lilt of Colleens in song,
There no other can ever compare,
'Tis of Ireland I'm speaking from tip to the toe,
Dungannon to Kerry so fair.

Though people travel to far and wide,
And settle on far distant shore,
They never forget the land of their birth
And stories of old folklore.
Meadows and moorlands shrouded in mist,
You may hear the tinkling of song,
Of leprechauns, fairies and people that roam,
Calling to those that belong,
'Come home, come home, come home to Ireland
You fools in far-off lands,
For in this paradise there's a place for you,
Come home and make your stand.'

Verge

Brown Eyes

I look into your eyes and see
The look of love and affection -
But, 'tis not you I see,
but the pain of my own reflection.

I long to touch and hold you near,
And know that I can't - for within
Your gaze I can see my fear. A feeling, a sadness,
Within my look and your perception.

To see in your eyes of good times past,
Our life, our love, and our bond
That did not last.
Our world, the one that belonged to you and me.
I look into your eyes, it brings back so many
Memories you see.

The beautiful brown eyes of the girl I knew -
Looking back at me now,
From the woman that is you.

The times of joy and laughter we had,
All obscured when it all went bad.
I long to touch and still hold you dear,
But your love is lost in my cries.

Your beauty I can only behold,
When I look into your loving brown eyes.

Peter Cranswick

Fire

Leaping over plains,
Sweeping life away,
Killing everything in sight
And spreading day by day.

Burning at wood,
Chewing the bark.
Killing many bird
From sparrows to skylarks.

Staying in one place
Keeping us warm
But when we take it on
It will become a flaming swarm.

David Hassan Benhenni

Bright Side Inside

We should all look on the bright side
As inside's easier to be seen
If we keep each other in the dark
Things always will be a dream

So try and show the way my friend
To everyone you meet
And they will find an outcome
Which will make their lives complete

Then they can show their friends that are
And people like me and you
That they have found upon the bright side
And what they found inside was true

S C Matthews

The Answer

I might just have the answer
To all of your prayers
There is somebody out there
Someone who really cares

No sense of commitment
Upon which to act
No sense of reality
Nothing is a fact

We feel no sense of pity
And no sense of shame
Just wanton destruction
Which we treat as a game

We accept what we think is best
And won't accept the wrong
Even though we all know
That it won't last very long

No point to this rhyme you say
But I point out that which is true
And as you're on our planet too
It also concerns you

What do you see as you look in the mirror
Do you see the past
It seems to me you don't know now
That the die has already been cast.

Andrew Britton

Dying At The Wrong Time

You should have died sooner,
before we two stopped loving,
before we found we had nothing to share,
before we stopped being a pair,
before we drifted apart,
before you broke my heart.

But you have died
when separate ways and loneliness
have been my life too long.
Now
you do not even leave a space
in a life you once filled.

Ann Rust

The Urge To Cultivate

I can't get on in the garden yet
It's far too cold, the ground's too wet
I think the sun has left the sky
And March is nearly slipping by
I have this urge to wield the spade
My summer plans have long been made
Old gardeners say, 'Be patient - wait
Don't get yourself in such a state
For nature will decide just when
You'll start to garden once again'
Still, having planted I've no doubt
The snails will come and eat me out.

G Andrews

Believe In Yourself

Judge not yourself through hurt and pain,
For you are special and you are sane.
Hold on to your dreams, try not to cry,
Live not in despair by questioning why.

Live not in the past and leave it behind,
There are so many answers you will never find.
Be true to yourself, you're only one being,
If you wear a mask, you're hidden from seeing.

Don't be a pawn in the chess game they play,
Use all of your pieces, ignore what they say.
For when they say 'check' it's only your bait,
With success and happiness, you have 'checkmate'.

Let the head rule the heart, the tears will not flow,
When the sun is shining your shadow will grow.
Your lesson was learnt, there's no denial,
There are many that love you, be strong and *smile!*

Anthay

My Gem

It is but the jewel
that sparkles
and twinkles
the setting . . .
that merely cradles
you,
my baby,
my love,
my life
are the most precious jewel
in my life's setting
and . . .
so very priceless.

Jillian Nagra

Ocean Of My Mind

Upon the waves I drift aloft
In my mind's eye, the waves are soft
Within the ocean of my mind
I'm free from all that grip and bind

David Betts

One Life, One Chance

I never thought this would happen to me,
In one painful sweep I felt my life shatter,
A scarred name to forever hold me back,
I thought I had so much to give, so much to offer.

The wrath of the law grabbed me in its ugly hands,
An empty feeling smothered my frail body,
Like a pawn on a chess set I could hardly move,
I felt a cloud of disappointment rain over me.

One moment can change your whole world around,
When you least expect it you can be knocked off balance,
Sometimes life feels unfair, unjust,
In the end it comes down to you, your one life, one chance.

Deep down I forgot what really mattered,
If I could only go back and alter my fate,
Things could have worked out better or even be worse,
The past can't be fixed but the rest of my life is for me to create.

My hands may be tied but my head remains high,
A clean slate, a fresh start, an end to my self-destruction,
Today my youth ended, my irresponsibility destroyed,
While a part of me died, another began to blossom.

Chris Campbell

Present Tense

Can you burst a storm cloud with an axe,
Or spilt a hail stone with a feather?
Better then to just relax
Than concern yourself about the weather.

I can't change this wine to water,
Or buy immortality with gold.
Every day my years grow shorter,
But I don't think about growing old.

So the next time you feel sad my friend
Or think the path you walk unfair,
Consider life is not about the journey's end,
But this present moment
And the love you share.

David McConville

If I Should Die . . .

If I should die before my time please take me to familiar ground.
I'd like to lay my head with those who've gone before,
The people I had chanced to be with in my life.
To find myself with friends and family.
So if I die before my time, remember this, and take me to
familiar ground.
Just lay me down and let me be, just take me to familiar ground
And let me spend eternity.

Jean Mulroy

Abominable Snowman

I'm nine feet tall with a white hairy hide,
All upright and erect I stride, with arms by my side
All through the thick snow I stroll and slide,
Rare and alone and with pride
I'm glad my white camouflage has kept me safe and well
As I roam this cold, icy hell,
I'm even described with a pong,
I just don't know what it is I've done wrong.

A mystery and a freak they think I am,
But all I am is just a rare ape, not a man.
We're so few in number so why does man try to catch us?
Why don't they just leave us alone and forget us?
They follow my big-foot trail in the snow
They just don't know when to stop and let me go,

For all I want to be is left to roam and to live safe -
With my family in my home,
But man won't stop until he's found my hidden lair of ice and crystal
Until I'm shot dead with his rifle or his pistol.

Donato Genchi

The Echoes Of Your Chaos

I can feel your tension building
I sit as quietly as I can
You scream and shout, push me about
Is this what makes you feel like man?
You control me with your power
I'm designed to be afraid
You accuse me of having an affair
And you're the one that's been betrayed
You humiliate me in front of others
I look to the floor with shame
My opinion doesn't mater, you tower over
Yes, I suppose I'm the one to blame.
I submit to your authority
Your abuse is getting worse
This torture is slowly killing me
Is this all that I am worth?
My cuts and bruises have healed now
But the emotional pain still hurts
He says to me, 'I cannot leave.'
And that he will kill me first.
How can I get help and tell others
When he has convinced me, 'It's not all that bad,
It will never happen again
There's no need to look so sad.'
You tell your friends it's all my fault
It must be my imagination
You put me down, throw me around
Restrain with intimidation
You control all my thoughts and feelings
It's natural to me somehow
You're begging for my forgiveness
I believe in you somehow.

Lucy Campbell

They Remember

As they approached the beach at dawn
The silence of the night had gone,
When they looked at each other they knew the score
They still can hear the cannons roar.

On this land they all did pray,
'Twas just another fighting day,
As time went by, they had no fear,
It went on daily, year by year.

As they crept quickly up a hill
They saw the people they had to kill.
As they fought bravely, the hours went by,
For most of them, some friends did die.

The sky was red by day and night,
The sight of dead people was such a fright,
As days went by, up on the hill
Such noise of guns, they can hear them still.

Down the road they all marched well,
Friend said to friend, it was *bloody hell,*
As the battle raged on and they neared the top,
Each wondered if this war would stop.

It drove them slowly round the bend,
They wished this war would come to an end.
On hill and streets, where we now play,
There is at last *peace*, we all can say.

George Collins

Stillborn

My heart goes out to you my friend
For I too have lost a child,
It may be many years ago
But memories go on file

I did not see her tiny face
Nor did I hear her cry,
And this will always stay with me
Until the day I die

I often feel her near me
In the softness of a breeze,
And in the centre of a flower
So aptly named Heartsease

It does no good to ponder
On what life might have been
If she had stayed to live her life,
It's just a long daydream

We can cry and question forever
But what good would it do?
Anniversaries bring a reminder
Mine total forty-two

Oh my heart goes out to you my friend
Whose tears from heartache flow,
Your child will live within your heart
Wherever you may go.

A Smedley

Never Alone

Angel feathers remind me
I'm never really alone,
Because God has made provision for me,
With an angel all of my own!

My angel is sent to guide me,
To help me when I ask,
And record my whole life story,
So as to repeat again when asked.

Though I struggle to see my angel,
And my ears don't always hear,
There's a feeling that stays inside me
And I know I need not fear.

Anne Helena Matley

A Prayer For Today

The world would be a better place
For people who were needy,
If everyone shared what they had,
Instead of being greedy.
Peace on Earth should be our aim,
Wars would be no more.
Not for the privileged; riches and fame,
Remember the needs of the poor.
The strong would lift the weak,
The rich would clothe the poor,
The healthy would nurse the sick,
The hungry *would* have more.
If everyone thought long and hard,
The purpose of our living,
Held *all* people in high regard,
Were gentle, caring and giving,
God would feel so proud to be
Our Father here on Earth,
If our actions made Him see
The reason for our birth.
So all peoples of the world unite,
Strong hands, one heart, one voice,
Let us put our wrongs to right,
In Lord Jesus we rejoice.

Marion Brown

Lifeboat!

Cross the road and rubble, drag the lifeboat free;
'There's a yacht in trouble with a crew of three!'
'Mick, help the cox'n aboard.'
'Quick, slip the ropes, get unmoored.'
Throttle at the double, we head out to sea.

Through the breakers smashing; there's a rising swell.
Hear the water splashing in the lifeboat's well.
Rush through a gale storm force five,
Must get those folk back alive!
Feel the bow waves crashing, as we go like hell.

It has been a long ride when the craft we see;
But we're on the wrong side, they must have our lee.
Blast! Little time we have got.
Fast, turn to circle the spot.
Once we are alongside, we retrieve all three.

Still the waves come roaring and our vessel rolls.
How the seas come pouring. 'Jack, avoid those shoals!'
'See, the yacht sinks out of sight.'
We pass the old harbour light:
Now the crew are mooring and we've saved all souls.

In some shady cavern free from stress and strife,
Or in harbour tavern where the jokes are rife,
We tell of storms and the slack;
One day we may not come back.
To the sea life given, for the sea's our life.

F Jeffery

I'll Be Back!

Circling gulls wheel and screech
    O'er the near deserted beach -
A few hardy visitors drink the dregs
    From autumn's cup which winter begs,
Along the windswept promenade,
    Shuttered, bolted down and barred
Are the hot dog stalls and those of ice cream sellers,
    Graffiti smeared by drunken revellers,
Soon will inclement winter come,
    The flesh to freeze and bones to numb,
And with its peculiar glut of ills,
    Lay folk low with colds and chills . . .
Ah well, it's time I was on my way,
    Take one last look across the bay,
The circling gulls will still wheel and screech
    Across the near deserted beach . . .
Until the sun returns, and birds will sing -
    That's when I will come again . . . in the spring!

F R Smith

Cricket

What did I know about the game of cricket?
Eleven men, a ball, and a thing called a wicket.
LBW and 'out for a duck'
Howzat, was the cry, oh what bad luck.
The batsman 'walked' no more fame
In fact he hung his head in shame.
Bowled and rolled, a boundary, a four
Silly mid on, flat on the floor
The ball's in the air, ripe for a catch.
The fans hold their breath, what a good match!
Bloody hell fire, short leg has dropped it.
The captain's not happy, he's having a fit.

The next batsman is big and he's fat,
His nickname is 'Biffer', but he can't half bat.
Over the wall, going for six, we don't need a silly umpire's tricks.
Short leg and fine leg, I've seen some of that,
The field is good, but can they bat?
Beamer, outlawed a dangerous delivery, down to the bowler
Well I beg to differ.
Quite often you know umpire's all of a dither.
A dodgy decision can 'B****r things up.'
Thumped and stumped will not win the cup.
So keep your heads lad, avoid a 'Yorker' in the block hole.
Give it slogs boys, play the role.

Cracking sixes and fours, don't give the oppo a chance.
You all lead them a merry dance.
Trust in your keeper, square leg, mid off and mid on.
The slips and the covers, the game will go on.
Victory is yours if the team can last.
Forget all the bad scores, it's all in the past.
Play well and hard and remember good passes.
You will probably then, bring home the ashes.

Ellen Spiring

My Hobbies

My hobbies are photography, knitting, writing poetry, my dog Pip,
and that is the lot,
So I combined them all together and this is what I got.

Pip poses for the camera, while I take photographs galore.
I develop them myself, and then I take some more.

I enjoy writing poems which are humourous and fun.
I have entered competitions and sometimes I have won.

Pip has a jumper for every occasion through the year.
She can turn up anywhere, wearing her fancy gear.

So there are my hobbies all rolled into one.
I hope I have not bored you with what I have done.

If you are bored, and you are sat on your Jack,
Take up a hobby, you will never look back.

Barbara Russell

The Sea

I hate the sea
for its evil and deceit.
I recall how it welcomed you,
while gently enticing you away from me.
So cunning, in not revealing its true intentions
I watched the sea play with you
like a cat does its prey.
Why did it grab you
and hug you so tight?
Leaving me breathless
and you without breath.

Ian Benjamin

Just An Ordinary Man

In all the years of history
To me no real mystery
It was those who stood to lose
And always the common man they chose
He was put in front to be the sentry
To fight the battles, for those with plenty
The common man, who could not run
In our hands they put a gun
Win or lose, only they who stood to gain
It was the common man who felt the pain
It was always us who had to do or die
Our wives and children, left to cry
Those of means, they did not care
They did not have to go, they did not dare
Our fathers died, and so may we
In all those years why did we not see
The common man has no foe
When next they ask, we should not go
Win or lose, we are left to die
There will be no time for tears, for us to cry

Francis McGarry

Thoughts Of Home

If I could have one moment now,
Captured real, of times before,
I'd give with all my heart to see
England's fields in spring once more.

To see the sunlight's gentle fall
On pastures green, on daffodil,
To walk the lanes and woodland paths,
To hear at wake the songbird's call.

But with truth, I must see
And vanquish forms of pleasantry,
For now in all a harshness be,
Where death becomes reality.

If damned we be, and all be gone,
Within this life of many wrongs,
My thoughts be not as one alone,
For all us lads have dreams of home.

Though cross this waste, with peril be,
Through gunfire, shrapnel, muddy sea,
In constant thought of what will be,
In hope,
At ends, to see,
Our English home.

Maxwell Dunlop

Is She Still In The Tower?

if ever her head hasn't got holes in it now
it never will have after the last six months nights

actually done so you can't repaint and write
what we have used of yours

besides the terrible pain
no one has ever been treated as you have

I doubt anyone in concentration camp got that
you have astounded us a bit

our killers are taught not to care
go and sit quietly . . .

but sirs it is the year of the chicken
and my sign is the cockerel

and it Is my nature to crow
though I do not fight or cause harm

to anyone.

Renate Fekete

Untitled

As daytime now ends and the dark clouds sigh
Bugles sing sombre and sad deep refrain
For thousands of brave men that war does try
Regret many of them will die in pain.

Now as they repose on beds of vile straw
With the night alive with such moaning pain
Sane men are besot with the sights they saw
Dreams they dream at night and yet thrice again.

Fear spoke saying 'You are weary and worn'
But the soldiers were not willing to stay
Battle they resumed at early morn
With valour and God's will to win the day.

Morning, after death had kissed life's shore
It left and in its wake; desolation
The entire world had bled and so they swore
To live once more in peace: as God's creation.

Leslie de la Haye

In Praise Of May

White candle flowers reach towards the azure sky
Their green skirts sway in the gentle breeze;
And sunshine glints through heavy laden bough
The chestnut tree heralds the month of May.

Beneath, shy pansies lift sweet faces to the sun:
Brilliant colours harmonise in many hues
So gentle flowers of tenderness and love
Rejoice to greet the loveliness of May.

The field beyond so fresh from morning dew
A playground for the gamboling woolly lambs.
The ewes watch, listening to the bleating calls
As ewes and lambs welcome the warmth of May.

And in the trees within the nest is heard
The cheep, cheep, cheep of blackbirds newly hatched.
The parent birds sing sweetly to their young
And with their song they praise the month of May.

The children laugh, and like the lambs they play
They sing as sweetly as the joyous birds.
Sweet faces raised like pansies to the sun
And in true harmony they join the chestnut tree in praise of May.

Barbara Dunning

Astrology

Astrology is the name of the game.
Stargazers - astrologists - fan the flame.
To part with your money is the aim.
Readings; forecasts; more the same;
Offer guidance to Fortune's dame.
Love - Luck - disasters tame;
Overall - predict life's frame.
Grief-stricken; lonely; sick or lame;
The lack of their 'luck charms' is to blame.

Buy my 'lucky heather',
'With silver, cross my palm.'
You've a kind face lady,
Buy this lucky charm,
Let me read the Tarots;
Gaze into my crystal ball.
Guide you through your future
Come. I will tell you all.

Time passes and you'll later find
That you've survived your pain.
Without that lucky win foretold;
That was the gazer's gain.
But, if by chance you do believe
In any of the above;
It is your fault if they deceive
And you forget God's love.

Barbara P Paxman

Swallows

Like darting fish
flashing in the shallows -
they trawl the slack;
swallows.

They come in waves
with fins for wings
to fish the ocean-sky -

trawl their catch;

suck their minnows dry.

Marc Harris

The Roaring Sea

Listen to the sound of the roaring sea,
calling out to you and me.
The waves roll in and spread out wide,
then disappear to leave a tide.
The sea can be calm and inviting,
bidding all to come in and see;
but whoever you are, don't go far,
or you will belong to me.
I can be frothing with anger,
throwing my waves upon the shore;
and each time you try to ride my waves,
I will toss you all the more.
Listen to the roar of the mighty sea,
I'm calling out to you looking back at me.
I'll cool you down when you're hot,
and I'll soothe your aching feet;
after you have been playing on my sand
in the soaring heat.
Remember to take your rubbish with you,
and don't chuck it in me;
keep the sand environmentally friendly,
and that includes the sea.

T Gibson

Pregnant Pause

The last leaves brave the winter cold,
Steadfast they cling to the tree,
Clothing it thinly in amber and gold
Before the cruel wind sets them free.

Then winter will have claimed its right to reign,
Trees will sway desolate and bare,
Frailty of limbs exposed for months
To the harshness of the numbing air.

At times they look so ugly and wizened,
Can they ever regain their splendour?
But, in the stillness of the winters' chill,
It's but a pregnant pause from November.

Buds are swelling beneath the bark
That covers each tapering spine,
The sap still flows to feed new life
Which will emerge when God gives the sign.

Then behold the glory of another spring,
Buds, blossom, leaflets so green
Clothing the dark, shivering, skeletal frames,
Trees become the backdrop to set the spring scene.

Pat Heppel

Tsunami

A wave that crashed and broke their lives and all within its wake
Was this the hand of God or was it our mistake?
The Western world with chimneys tall, the greenhouse gas effect?
The other side of the world, their lives would still reflect
For we've destroyed the ozone layer, we take and don't put back
And people who are dying are paying for our lack
They didn't ask for fame or wealth and electric everything
We all have computers and mobile phones to ring
We've sapped all the energy out of this good Earth
And innocence will pay the price, it's been like it since our birth

Grace Divine

Seduced

I meant to work really hard today
But the sun seemed so glad to see me,
She asked waves to line-dance along the bay.
I smelt the air of a wonderful May.
Clouds rendered me powerless
So I followed, without much stress.
They seduced me to the beach where all
My work was out of reach.

J W Whiteacre

Pride Blooms

I'd love to write a poem
About a garden filled with blooms.
The sunflower with the tallest stem
And the pampas reminds me of plumes.
Now the pansy has a tiny face
And the snapdragon has a mouth,
The rose has lots of style and grace
And the bluebells are looking south.
A carnation is so frilly,
Just like a senorita's dress
And then there is the lily,
With colours so bright and fresh.
The lavender is so fragrant and fair,
But the poppy stands with pride,
So instead of a poem, I'll just say a prayer
In memory of the soldiers that died.

Shirley Jones Dwyer

Cold Friends

Winter wipes her muddy feet on dirty doormats everywhere.
Drumming rain and slicing sleet drizzle daily without fear.
Robin finds his closest perch on frozen fence, his trilling clear,
Singing for scraps of bread to eat, flung from kitchen doorways near.
Hedgehogs hide in bonfire heaps, nests they form with every care
Till sun returns with summer heat, no cold, no winter sleeping there.
Steps of curious animal feet, red deer slip from hillside sheer,
Food supplies depleted - they search for fodder - stomachs bare.
Feral claws release their sheath; wildcats play at solitaire,
Dustbin alley dining room, fangs howl hunger and despair.
If you find a sheltered beat, with feeding space for all to share,
Watch beauty in this winter street - when wildlife feed in frosty air.

Leigh Crighton

Far From The Meadow

Cut grass, sweet summer-scented, soothing, green,
Stirs inklings of a fierce primal past
Rooted beneath a pleasant garden scene . . .
Mow the lawn retired man,
Taming the grass that civilised you,
Far, far from the meadow where
Shoulder-high, the wild grasses grew,
Wheat-eared, barley-whisped, rye-sharp and rough,
Thrusting up, broad, coarse and strong
Blade after blade, tangled and tough;
Far, far from your forebear crouched for the kill,
His heart cold as the sharp stone in his hand,
Necessity keeping him rigid and still
Closing his mind to everything but
His immediate need of something to eat.
Didn't see beauty, didn't feel pity
For the wild creature bleeding at his feet.
Didn't notice the meadow's varied yield,
Quivering seed heads, fronded, shiny, smooth;
No vision of bread from a golden field,
A settled life and time to think and be;
His hunting ground a sunlit picnic place
Where people could sit contemplatively.
Ages and Ages of Stone would pass
Before his descendants discovered
The secrets of grass.
Centuries, millennia, between
The man with the mower
And him.

Pam Hatcher

Too Early For Autumn

The trees are sparse of leaves, this time of year,
And upon the hedgerows strange crimson fruit appear
Like countless frozen droplets of blood,
Filled with the poison of millions of years.
In the spring, I saw you proud and strong,
Accompanied by your little sapling son,
A healthy pink blossomed in your face,
None could have beamed more a carefree grace.
But so cruel are the changing winds of fate,
When the peaceful breeze gathers pace.
Yet, no one was aware of the urgency,
For a gale was forming,
Its harshness unceasing in its frequency.
Dislodging the very colour from your boughs,
Turning before time
Every leaf from yellow to ashy-grey,
Cutting down in his prime,
A loving father fallen prey
To an early autumn which will not delay.
Within your shadow, and beside
A little boy will grow with pride
To know that he is of your seed,
Becoming in time, a good man indeed.

William Shaun Milligan

Secrets Of The Forest

(Dedicated to Alma and John Westwood)

In the vaulted forest the rain softly falls,
the tawny owl blinks and the wood-pigeon calls.
Deep within these cloistered glades,
where shadows thrive and sunshine fades,
voices whisper of promises broken,
of secrets never to be spoken.

Through stately pillars the bright loch shines,
like a mirror reflecting those lofty pines.
Brown water sleeps through the placid hours,
beneath a coverlet of gold lily flowers.
Home to nymphs and mischievous sprites
where fates are sealed on moonless nights.

The wee burn chatters to the ancient stones.
The black crow cries in raucous tones.
Does the sighing wind overhead
grieve for a friend long since dead?
Does the stranger, moved to tears,
mourn the passing of the years?

Beyond the loch does the soft grey mist
hide the ghost of a lover's tryst?
Who can remember the first bright dawn
before these mighty trees were born?
The secrets that haunt the forest floor,
will surely stay hidden for evermore.

Sonja F Mills

Winter Comes, But How Does It Go?

Winter is coming, it can't be far away,
Very much colder, but rain has gone today,
Too early to predict,
What the weather will inflict,
But many promise severe cold,
Not welcomed, when one is very old.

What are the scores,
For those confined indoors,
Fewer trips to the shops,
Heating supplement for them the tops,
But how will they spend the time
If the climate is not very kind?

Some may read, while others may knit,
Particularly those who are not quite fit,
Radio and television may some attract,
No conversation, if alone on the track,
For them, a visitor is most welcome,
Be it friend, or social worker, to come.

When on one's own time can drag,
Not knowing what next is in the bag,
Every minute can seem an hour,
Occupation not in everyone's power,
Slumber may be a delight,
But not if it extends the night.

So think of those who are confined,
Made even worse for one that's blind,
A chance to talk, all they need,
To pass the time, but not at speed;
Let's find the time to call someone,
In person, or even on a phone.

George Beckford

Acolyte

Holding its face up
to the source of creation,
the *girasol* turns:
Jerusalem artichoke -
sunflower by another name.

Norman Bissett

The Colour Of Seasons

Whirling past the windowpane
Down and round and round again,
Snowflakes light and airy fly
From a heavy laden sky.
Black and bleak the branches stretch,
Leaves and berries, beauty stripped
By icy wind and lashing hail
Sway to and fro in winter's gale.
Oh hurry spring! Oh soon break through,
Bring forth the crocus flowers anew.
The wallflowers, tulips, daffodil,
Soft sunshine leaving wind less chill.
May, June, July and brilliant sky,
Long lazy days of summer.
The scented stocks and hollyhocks
And evening breeze a whisper.
A landscape change - the painter's brush
Sweeps autumn on the scene.
The hills and fields seem in a rush
To change to gold from green.
So on and on the seasons go,
For all time and forever.
We write, we paint, we sing,
But oh!
The theme it changes never.

Doris Mary Miller

Beginnings

The door to all wisdom
Is deep in the mind
Yet, reveals unto none
But the truly inclined
Unto searching for something
May never they find
Leaving else, before wisdom
Behind

We're taken from a woman
And we're given from a man
We're living up to every day
But anyway we can
We're born beside our afterbirth
And slow to understand
That, all above the inner earth
Is just a lump of land

Let there be no countries, no colours, no gods,
No sacred possessions, nor hate!
No relative races at relative odds
And no promise of provident fate!

If that, we instil, shall we live by
And that, we instil, be all wrong,
Then that, that instil we
Shall conquer, and kill we
Till relative we's be all gone!

All our beginnings begin with the ends
Of another beginning's demise
Constructed by nature's destructible trends
And the secrets behind the surprise

As ever, when diminished so
Does hope become their fear
For only shall beginnings show
When finishings, appear!

Mark Anthony Noble

Sometimes

Sometimes I'm a graceful cloud,
Floating high, above all worries.
But sometimes I'm a grumpy blizzard,
Angry and strong, in huge flurries.

Sometimes I'm the glowing sunshine,
Smiling brightly on everyone,
But sometimes I'm the lonely moon,
On my own, without any fun.

Sometimes I'm a cheerful rainbow,
Colourful and confident, as if on stage.
But sometimes I'm a howling wind,
Disrupting everything in my rage.

Sometimes I'm a glittering star,
Shining, bright and even witty!
But sometimes I'm a dense fog,
Muggy and thick, *so* not pretty!

Sometimes I'm a clear blue sky,
Pleasing all the people I meet.
But sometimes I'm a dripping raindrop,
To ruin your day, and dampen your feet.

Katie Wood (15)

Dear Sir

I'm in need of an outlet
My poems are gathering dust
The tears of despair flow so freely
My cheeks are beginning to rust
My verses are rhyming and rhythmic
Naive and unpolished, some say
But 'Easy to read' is my slogan
And folk seem to like them that way
My ditties have met with approval
From relatives, neighbours and friends
And even my epics find favour -
But that's where the cheerful news ends
The experts, it seems, are offended
By light-hearted off'rings like mine
And yet I'm reluctant to change them
The truth is, they suit me just fine
And then a kind preacher suggested
'Try Anchor books - *that's* what to do'
And so I decided to round up
Some samples and send them to you
Best wishes, and thank you for reading
It could be I'll still make my mark
But if not, I'll welcome your comments

Yours faithfully,
Helen M Clarke

H M Clarke

My Heart Won't Cry

I close my eyes, a voice awakened my heart
With gentle words beauty and art
Like a statue to a spirit blessed
From sadness, tears the end of my quest

A sensual touch of warming calm
Flamed my passion with devoted charm
The shivering waves I treasure deep
For the love, romance, happiness, sleep

Gracefully striving down the river of time
Through rapids and falls we climb
Ups and downs, my life now bliss
With passion you planted the perfect kiss

The whispered secret you gave the key
Devoted passion that will stay with me
Until the day our souls do fly
My darling wife my heart won't cry.

R S Wayne Hughes

Remembering A Few Friends

He sits on a bench
surrounded by old friends,
he arrived here in style
in a posh Mercedes Benz.

He always arrives alone
he talks for hours,
then he leaves alone
placing a bunch of flowers.

It seems like yesterday
when they were all lads,
knowing they all died
just leaves him feeling sad.

As his Mercedes starts
and slowly pulls away,
that young man suddenly
feels so old and grey.

Carl Spencer

Dreams And Accomplishments

Pursuing the dreams in the avenues of life,
the path where uncertainty is rife,
and the future plans are completely cherished,
as if they would be soon accomplished.

The devastating situations try to refrain,
showing diversions to determined brain,
an unsteady brain asks again and again,
is it the path you did aim?

The hurdles that really challenge enthusiasm,
as if they just snap with sarcasm,
compelling one to face back and give up,
but it's not so easy when the lungs are puffed up,

The passioned desires tackle difficulties,
as they believe, 'there are limited opportunities'
when they succeed they respect the loyalties
else they console, there are many opportunities

Several factors make one confused,
but one should be rigid what he chose
the hurdles of the path are not permanent
be ambitious to change a dream to accomplishment.

Himanshu Kardam

Like Cinderella, Or Spenser

Like Cinderella whom cruel others drive
Sadness through with no concern except their own,
She dressed to please that night, but could not thrive
As appearance was never wholly known.
The ship she would sail with timbered bones
Would break and ruin when humble thoughts appeared.
Her heart would tumble, the place heave and groan
Because others at the ball only leered.
She could sail on fast and briefly shatter her fear.

Sarah Taylor

Shattered Lives And Mended Spirits

As I awake each tearless morn and reflect upon my life,
I wonder I survived at all through conflict, pain and strife,
To tell the tale and spread some hope to the beaten and oppressed,
Who trudge the rocky road each day in north, south, east and west.

My childhood days were measured out in decibels of fear.
A verbal onslaught gauged as two when flavoured with a sneer;
A beating far exceeded this when it ruptured the fragile skin,
Taking parasitic hold of me with a permeating din.

I know there must be thousands still who suffer in this way,
Young minds fall foul to sabotage every dreaded day,
Bodies that have been defiled or beaten to a pulp,
Children so invisible they're too afraid to gulp.

For each of the tormented the world will also hold,
A wicked, wasted tormentor who outwardly seems bold.
But can you really comprehend why the bravest of them all,
Would persecute the vulnerable with a nauseating thrall?

It's a sign of inner cowardice, the mark of someone weak,
To lord it over others with their inherent nasty streak.
Try to hold this thought at the forefront of your mind;
You are not to blame for this, and with time you'll find

An inner strength to call on, support from someone who
Will help to turn your life about and show you what to do.
There are thousands of good people who populate this earth,
Turn to one of them and start to realise your worth.

Alison Adams

Diets

I've decided to start a diet today
it's something I decide but always delay
food seems much nicer when you're watching your weight
the trouble is I'm getting fatter so just can't wait!

Chocolate, crisps and cakes are a no go
sadly I'm now beginning to feel quite low
I regret putting all my treats in the bin
must keep reminding myself they are a sin!

Thinking about it a size 8 is far too small
perhaps I'm just being a silly fool!
It's good to have some fat on your frame
wearing a size 12 shouldn't fill me with shame!

My resolve is now beginning to break
the willpower I had developed is beginning to shake
one piece of chocolate really won't hurt
as long as I'm still able to fit in my skirt!

Oh well that's it, I've eaten it all
the chocolate's all gone, I'm in for a fall!
Never mind there's always tomorrow
the whole diet experience seems to fill me with sorrow!

Karen Wileman

Rumour

Rumour tempts a fool to judge
The nod, the wink, the grin, the nudge
A clean-cut image, smear and smudge
Without exception,
From honest grit to man-made sludge
Come this election.

David Russell McLean

You

(Dedicated to my wife Debbie)

You are my faith, I am the meek
You are my strength when I am weak
You give me hope when I am lost
You come to my aid whatever the cost
You are the sunlight shining on my face
You are my angel that grants me grace
You put the warmth back in my heart
You lift me up when I fall apart
You showed me love when I was blind
You led the way I could not find
You saw the love that was in my eyes
You are my goal, you are my prize.

Peter Ramsden

Hurting

Scarred for life,
You left your mark
Right down the middle of my heart.

The fault still bears upon the barren lands of my hear,
The phoenix's tear, no competition, the pain will prevai.
It still hits me like a tranquilliser dart,
The day when you left me beneath my veil.

Guilty of never saying what I truly felt,
And now I see that it's too late.
One look at your eyes would make me melt,
That look that I now have begun to hate.

Life ticks away, time stands still,
Bruising my soul, making me ill,
Can you feel it, can you feel the pain?
What I have lost, you have to gain.

Tick-tock the ever-haunting sound of that clock.
It's mocking me, with every tick and every tock.
It knows you left me standing,
It knows you left me hurting.

Lorna Forbes

Star Wars

Moon is the official icon of romance
With mesmerising wax-wane dance
Ah it is not the moon but the stars
That raise and lower romance bars

Political stars promise the moon
That waxes late but wanes soon
Candidates lining up exclusive dinners
Becoming exclusive once declared winners

Sports stars promise honeymoon
Thrill-a-minute romantic swoon
Combining well personal pride
With emotional patriotic ride
Wowing us with on-field feats
But stardom brings off-field beats

Cine stars promise to be blue moon
More romantic than Mills & Boon
Flooring us with performance real in reel
But after a hit behaves reel in real

Aha the twinkling little stars
God's own cookie jars
Real romance-rousers, steady and straight
Shining the same night after night

Ohoo dears there is a catch
Better wear chemistry patch
Look up with right partner - heart
They sure tingle a body part
Becoming brighter beacons of romance
Wink, whisper, make the soul dance

Oh boy . . . choose the wrong handle
They whine worse than candle
Opening the trap for you and me
To prefer astrology to astronomy
Oh trusting false stars for future dance
We begin the last rites of romance.

S M Sivaraman

Last Will And Testament

Who will wipe my tears when I grow old
Or pick me up and not be told?
Who will smile and nod their head
And not understand a thing I said?
Who will give me drugs and pills
For all my dreadful lingering ills?
Who will hear my ultimate breath
And close my eyes on final death?

I do not search for such a fate
While waiting for the pearly gate
The fear and hate for such an ending
Is ever there in thoughts now pending
So here and now I make my plea
To whoever watches over me
When I am lost and far from mind
Flick the switch and be so kind.

Sam Kelly

Two Young Spirits Flying Free

Dancing on a crystal sea,
Their laughter breaks upon the shore,
Their silver voices rise and soar.

Soon they're leaping over breakers,
Rhythmic waves like orchestral shakers,
Crashing down in perfect time,
The beautiful sound of nature's rhyme.

Now they're playing on the beach,
A simple lesson they can teach,
To just let go all inhibition
Is their carefree childhood mission.

Whirling over pebbled dunes
Releasing dusty, sandy plumes,
Chasing, catching, hiding, finding,
Are two young spirits together binding.

Forever sisters, forever friends,
Forever in this world of pretend,
Where they will share such memories
Of summer's fun in sea-blown breeze.

And two together can be one
Under the smiling summer's sun,
Remembering when times were easy
And childhood games were long and busy.

Then when they are grown and their spirits are low,
Their memories will show them where to go,
Back to where they had not a care,
Where dreams were what two sisters shared.

Laura Crean

A Tribute To Carers

I wonder if you realise
Just how we see you through our eyes?
A carer is the one to know
Our final days of pain and woe.
From owner down to learner-lass
She cares for everyone she has.
She shares with us a frequent visit,
We ring the bell. 'Yes dear, what is it?'
It matters not how tired she feels,
How oft the shrill alarm peals,
She quickly calms the agitator,
With, 'Okay darling, see you later.'
Your Home has really got to be
More than a cold efficiency.
We thank you for the love you're sharing
So bless you carers, keep on caring.

Margaret Thorpe

Siren Song

As I was sitting down by the bay,
Three lovely mermaids came my way,
'Come in,' they trilled in their siren song,
'Come in, come in, come in.'
I stood up and plunged into the bay,
I searched and searched, 'Which way, which way?'
'Down, down,' came the sirens' cry,
I looked in vain, saw nothing with my eye,
Then suddenly my senses blurred,
I floated back up to Mother Earth,
Alas, the trio had done their worst,
My lungs had filled, fit to burst,
No more will I sit down by the bay,
Passing all the daylight hours away.

Don Antcliff

Unspoilt

Petals fall through a world
of curves and lines
lights that collect so
bright at night
yet fade
when she comes
they rose to meet her
then collapsed away.
For how lovely are our days.

George Jones

A Horse's Dream

Wild, majestic, born to be free,
jumping over fence and tree,
hooves-a-galloping over grass,
over mountains, through rocky pass,
Splash through rivers, brooks and streams,
every horse's wildest dream.

Mane is streaked and eyes are bright,
the stallion runs throughout the night,
cantering for hours and hours,
through sun and wind and rain and showers,
trotting on till journey's end,
rider's steed and greatest friend.

Joanna Boyd

A Song For Summer

Meandering meadows, sparkling streams
Summer's here, or so it seems
Nature returns to living hues
And birds at daybreak sing the news

Golden sands and calming seas
Swooping gulls glide on the breeze
Men in whites, cricket pavilion
Tourists flocking by the million

Filing past at fairground rides
Bouncy castles, bumpy slides
Bronzing children play all day
Then dream sweet dreams, the night away

Boat trips down the roaming river
(Excitement's all to make us shiver)
Families having so much fun
Quality time out in the sun

Lovers walking in the park
Picnicking until it's dark
Easy life, seems trouble free
Cares all gone, so come with me . . .

Melinda Penman

Tears May Stream

You're so tired, been travelling for so long,
Searching for answers,
You still can't believe they've gone.

Years of torture etched on your face,
Seeing you suffer,
My life a mess, yours is a waste.

Torn between life and death,
Stood by their side watching on,
Regret in your voice, with every breath,
Nobody there, they've already gone.

Holding hands throughout the pain,
Moments lost, never regained.
The words of a text,
What's in store, what's next.

Flashbacks, a knife and blood,
I'd ease the pain if I could.
Regret, remorse, angst, sorrow,
Through your veins it will flow.

Your silent screams,
Your distant dreams.
These wounds won't heal,
The lost childhood you did steal.

Happy people, infectious smiles,
Reassurance from across the miles.
Strength emergent after all,
The hurt you caused, the heart you mauled.

Jane Tomlin

My Daughter, My Cooper And I

I love my Mini and my mini-me
They are my world and more
They are cheeky and nippy and love to be
By my side so I can fully adore.

Paula Hartley

Fred's Fate

I was a little budgie.
My name was Fred.
I lived in a little cage,
And wished that I was dead.

My wings had never taken flight.
No friends for company.
No toys for stimulation,
Such a lonely destiny,

They put me in a cardboard box
And took me out one day,
Back to the pet shop,
While they went on holiday.

I never reached the pet shop.
My owner dropped my box.
I escaped forever
The chains, the bars, the locks.

I flew up to a chimney pot
And viewed a world so wide.
The breeze blew freedom, space and life.
My bosom heaved with pride.

I met a little tabby cat.
She said I was a winner.
I trusted her until she
Ate me for her dinner!

Wendy Preece

Zulu

The Zulu army swept down from the hill
The sergeant said, 'Fire at will.'
'Which one of them's Will,' I said with a start
'Don't worry son, just aim for the heart.'

'Aim for the heart,' I said with a grin,
'These Zulu warriors are so tall and thin.'
'Calm down son, this thing is quite clear,
Each one of them is carrying a spear.'

'Spear,' I said, 'aren't they quite sharp,
By twelve o'clock I could be playing a harp.'
Reload your rifle, get ready to shoot,
The sergeant's orders we must execute.

The Zulu army crept over the ground.
We'd have to fight to the very last round.
Stacking the sandbags to form a defence,
The Zulu army was looking immense.

Surrounded by Zulus as they close in,
The odds are against us, we may not win.
Time after time reload and aim,
Picking them off, like hunting game.

Wave after wave of Zulus attack.
Firing our rifles stood back to back,
Protecting the fort from being overrun.
Fighting the Zulu in the baking hot sun.

Brian Williams

My First Love

A cycle was the stead on which he rode,
His legs were long, and tanned, and very strong.
Abundant wavy hair he had, so dark.
Was this the knight for whom I'd waited long?
I felt I was a clumsy village girl
Without a dress to wear, or funds to spend.
The club of youths and girls was thriving well;
Relationships were there to break and mend.
He was attracted to me it was clear,
My confidence and joy began to swell.
I watched, and longed for him to speak to me,
Was this a real romance? How can you tell?
He seemed to be so old, I just a teen,
And yet there were but four years in-between.

Janice Ginever

Roots

'Apple pie without cheese,
Is like a kiss without a squeeze.'

Thirty years of living in the south,
And my Yorkshire roots I still reveal,
By the food I place within my mouth.

Charles Christian

What's In A Nickname

A poser in the post was sent
Three names to tease and tantalise,
So every day some time I spent,
To find a clue and centralise
Upon a theme quite humorous,
Which might explain the reason why,
Majestic names quite glamorous,
Sit sadly on the smallest fry
And so, with colleagues I conferred,
Based on the English attitude,
When nicknames sometimes are preferred
And welcomed, with great gratitude.

A daughter could most Lovely be,
Perhaps a pretty Prettie too,
A Sweetie also possibly,
Though sons are sweet and lovely too,
Especially when they rally round
The practicalities of day,
Oblivious of songs that pound,
Our peace and sanity away,
These names I'll now evaluate,
Sweetie and Lovely are female,
Upon Prettie, I'll cogitate
And guess, perchance, this is a male!

Lorna Troop

Untitled

Do you ever dream of me?
In the long dark nights,
When all is still,
And thoughts are our own,
When events gone past,
Revisit just one more time?

Do you ever think of me?
When you're all alone
Remembering what we could have had,
If life and fate had left us,
To live and love more carelessly?
I do, on the nights when sleep evades,
And my thoughts turn to what might have been.

Helen Goode

Soon As

Need to see you, feel you, hold you
Have to reach you, touch you, kiss you
Chat, talk, laugh, cry, get to know you
Loves, hates, wants, needs, here to show you
Want to find you, free you, bind you
Twinkle, glisten, dazzle, blind you.

Need to see me, rock me, reel me
Have to watch me, catch me, teach me
See, hear, smell, touch, get to know me
Hopes, fears, goals, dreams, there to show me
Want to own me, have me, share me
Take note, listen, challenge, dare me.

Gabrielle Gascoigne

Emily

Emily wants to do
All that I do
She forgets
She is still only three
She thinks she can
Kick a ball
Into a goal
But she can't
Even do it like me
If I say
Watch me Em
She jumps up and down
Thinks she knows
That whatever I do
She's as good as me
Mind you she dresses herself
So I guess
She's a little like me.

Jeanette Gaffney

They Think They Know Me!

Can people imagine
How I really feel?
Do they honestly think
My feelings they can steal?

What makes people think
They even understand me?
Are there things, I don't know,
They feel, they can show me?

Such foolish thoughts,
Can they see inside my head?
Do they know, what troubles me,
As I lay on my bed.

When I wake in the morning,
Do people know, what I reach for?
Some peace of mind,
I can't find anymore.

I know what I want,
I'm desperate for affection.
But deep inside,
There is a fear of rejection.

But I go, with my instincts,
That gut feeling inside.
So let these words tell you,
I don't want to hide.

Daviydh

The Dolphin Show

I see some dolphins jump through hoops,
Then I see them jump through loops.
They swim around in a pool,
I think they're really cool.
They do some tricks
And give people licks.
One of the dolphins smile at me,
And I smile back with plenty of glee.
Now it's time to go,
I really enjoyed the show.
I really want to stay,
For the rest of the day.
But I really must go,
Because I need to get home.

Sarah Festa (10)

When I Think Of Autumn I Think Of . . .

Damp, cold nights,
Howling, whistling winds,
Crispy, crunchy leaves,
New, fresh harvest,
Short, dull days,
Exploding, dashing fireworks,
Sleepy, hibernating animals,
Tasty, juicy fruits,
Shiny, hard acorns,
Spiky, hazel chestnuts.

Aisling Cullen (10)

Tonight's Not The Night For Missing You

12.53am

Tonight, I'll give myself a simple gift
And give it simply too -
I'll tell myself that I've done well
And not think that it's untrue.

2.18am

Tonight, I'll give my heart a break
And break it slightly too -
I'll think about the future now,
And not of missing you.

Jonathan Curtis

You Draw My Smile With Starlight

You are the snowdrops on the sunlit mountains
an angel dancing in the sky,
you are the luminescence of a silver sun
the calmness of a lullaby,
you are the sapphire savannah in my opaque dreams
a hypnotic, narcotic within my mind,
you are a golden puzzle to perplex my thoughts
the iridescent waterfalls in the stillness of time
you are frozen music chiming amid glass shadows
an ocean ebbing away past pain,
you are a kaleidoscope of evergreen sincerity
the beautiful colours from a bow of rain,
you are this endless imagery my warm heart conveys
an aura of timeless inspiration,
you are the reason these words grace the page
the perfect picture of pure perfection . . .

Mathew Cullum

Let Not Sadness Show

With time in my soul this hour of the day,
this void would be filled if you were to stay.
Then kindness comes forth with a smile on its face,
for love is a moment in this hour of grace.
Let not sadness show in parting my love,
for life is an arena filled with sounds from above.

Give to my heart that blessing of touch,
so that I can feel love, it means so much.
Then by my return I will pursue this dream,
on flight from my soul like the rippling stream.
Content will be I, knowing this void will be filled,
then love's own sweet story of no sadness be told.

The smile in your voice and love on your lips,
will caress me so sweetly as time gently slips.
Past those hours when we are apart,
waiting and wanting that blithe spirit to start.
That brief encounter, that touch of your hand,
to be held in your arms with a love that is so grand.

John Clarke

Home And Away

At first it was all about performance
touching and lasting, satisfying
and coming in both body and soul
talking nonsense through the early hours,
then she wanted space
as if she saw me as a human straight jacket
and went off on her own
and the empty chill of solitude was mine once more
addressed and posted by fate to my door
then within seconds hope returned
like sun's rays through corn
her voice high on hope and expectation
came over the phone
wanting me or something deep inside
my inner being I may not really know
or recognise, as being familiar
and once again she will play me like a flute
until I am dry
and free from doubt - for now!

Laurence DE Calvert

Lost Love

There's a pain in my heart
That cannot be filled
It stirs up a storm
That cannot be stilled

It's now that you've gone
I miss you the most
But you got your call up
And answered your post

I remember the day
The letter arrived
It read of the news
That you hadn't survived

Now the war it is over
But time heals they say
But my broken heart
Never mends till this day.

Karen Christie

Dear Mother Goodnight

In laughter I knew her
and knew her so well
all for my mother
my love I did tell

she could be angry
and scolding as well
when the youngest of four
a miscreant did tell

but always she loved me
and always she cared
as dark clouds a sky filled
and courage despaired

knowledge she had not
she knew it was so
the mind of her son
a smartness did show

how shall I praise her?
in verse I shall write
I owe her my thanks
dear mother goodnight.

George Carle

The Most Ugly Garden Of All

I grew some beauty.
Like a flower at the end of the world.
Found in a pool of moonlight.
In colourless dreams,
You had the colour of drained cheeks.
The moth surrounded your illumination.
And those succulent, water petals glowed.

This is my garden, I weeded all the others.
Until, only you were standing.
I watered and nourished the only beauty.
But when the season comes,
It will bring your death.
Then there will be nothing left.

Hayley Nix

Darkness Of The Night

The sky is raining feathers
From an angel's broken wings
As pieces of her glass heart
Fall down upon broken strings
On a golden harp from Heaven
That will no longer serenade
Harmonies of true love
As voices slowly fade
Memories on sharded glass
The mirror of her heart
Lie upon the hardened ground
Such beauty torn apart
Betrayal walks without a care
As cruelty leads the way
This dark night of the soul that runs
The one she tries to save
But her light within his darkness
Is lost amidst the void
Her love, her heart, her mind, her soul
His darkness has destroyed
But one day he will awaken
From the solitude world where he sleeps
Cloaked in hate and self pity
Where eyes of stone never weep
And remember the kiss of an angel
And the love she brought with the light
Trying so hard to free his soul
From the darkness of the night.

Lisa Jane Mills

Picaresque

Your eyes twinkle like stars
Your smile rosy and bright

Full of fun
For charity you run

Generous to a fault
Never know when to halt

Cancer you bore
Your womb no more

Your silent pain
Shooting through my vein

Lighthouse rotating light
For passing ships in the night.

John McCartney

Sheila

As dappled cobalt shadows run
From golden as the midding sun,
Wild the wooded flower grows.

Gentle rock the breezing boughs.

Amid the blue tits come and go,
Wild the wooded flowers grow
Deep beneath the azure sky,
All Heaven's lapis lazuli . . .

. . . Sheila barefoot walks the stream,
Picking bluebells from a dream . . .

In silver bark jade dragonfly
Waft that lapis lazuli,
That kingdom of the little bell,
That Heaven of the silent knell.

Roger Mosedale

Greed

Champagnes, steaks
we like the taste
but some's left over,
it's only waste.

Foreign hols, a flashy car
a fancy sounding job;
unless you have just one of these,
you're just a social slob.

A choice of clothes
a choice of shoes.
What shall I wear?
What shall I use?

Credit cards or easy terms,
help buy the latest need.
But is it really needed
or is it simple greed?

Videos and tellies
hi-fis, answer phones
these things are all around us
in our fully furnished homes.

But do we really need them,
these so called homely things,
or is it the social status
that having them will bring?

Simon Martin

Nothing Up His Sleeve

The postmodernist magician
doesn't stoop to trickery -
he uses thought-waves and conditions,
employs mystic 'philosophies'.

No attending famulus
assists him with his sleight of hand
when one TV appearance
gladly pays a hundred grand

to plug his latest situation
and make love to the camera.
He's on every other station,
screwing with the media:

no scarves, no doves, no playing cards -
it's the twenty-first century!
No arcane secrecy to guard,
no sense of mystery.

From the golden age, one frippery
our magician still adheres:
large amounts of currency
appear, then disappear.

Bruce McRae

Samurai And Masai

One Samurai drinks sake
When he is sad,
And has the mania
To smoke cigarettes.
Samurai comes in Kenya
By invitation of his friend Masai.
Masai meets the old friend Samurai.
Samurai turned red
From the heat
Begins to smoke a cigarette.
Coal-black Masai turns yellow-green
From the tobacco smoke-screen!
Ignorant of Japanese language Masai
Suddenly speaks to Samurai:
'Tabacco-o goenryo kudasai!' *

* Please, no smoking!

Petr Nicolayevich Maltsev

Divorce

The fight is over, I've lost the battle and the war,
I'm living in a high rise flat on the second floor.
I have no option, things must change, look to pastures new,
a pub could be the answer, but landladies are few.

I've convinced the brewery, they've given me this gig,
I'm their first licensee, a bit of a guinea pig.
The pub's thriving, profits are high, doing very well,
but lonesome wives are knocking, with wicked tales to tell.

The demand, 'Return their men', the boycott has begun,
with posters and pickets, they're telling everyone.
It's a house of ill repute, no one must go inside,
cowering behind closed doors, afraid to step outside.

The business is in ruins, had to admit defeat,
frightened of being homeless? Living on the street?
A quick call to the council, another high-rise offer,
a wine shop, a vacancy, wages for the coffer.

Interview over, now we can move into the flat,
time to look to the future, a place to hang my hat.
Fate at last smiles upon me, after a shaky start,
a salary, a roof. Much more a contented heart.

Marian Cutler

Techno-Prat

'It's broken,' they said
But I just shook my head
As they viewed their PC in dismay
Some rank amateur's hand
Their computer had jammed
I was confident I'd save the day
'It just needs rebooting,' I said
Executing my misinformed technical skills
So I blithely jumped in with a 'child's play' type grin
And the footwear to cure such ills
To reboot a PC is quite simple you see
For those with the requisite knowledge
Turn it off at the main
Turn it back on again
But I'd failed my IT course at college
So I thought it meant
(I've no technical bent)
A swift kick up the chip was required
With my left foot drawn back
I gave one mighty whack
And the PC, in flames, then expired
Here's the moral to this
If there's something amiss
With anything technically sound
Most important of all
Get an expert to call
Don't discuss it if Ron is around.

Ron Beaumont

Rhyming Mouse

Tick-tick, tick-tick
It nicely rhymes with click
Tock-tock, tock-tock
A grandfather clock . . .

The mouse ran down
The clock struck one
Then stopped, for
Gravity was out of space.

Click left, click right, clickety quick
The curser searching for a simple bite.
Click, quick - flick the switch and smile,
Then recall the mouse as a gnomon-shadow.

Chris Lobban

A Stunner

Angus and his friends
Were dining out one night
The waitress was a stunner
A captivating sight
A voluptuous beauty
Her blouse, the tightest fit
Wearing a short skirt
And legs that wouldn't quit!

She asked to take their order
As they sat wide-eyed
All were mesmerised
By the beauty at their side
'I'd like a quickie'
Ogled Angus, lacking grace
But she promptly slapped him
Hard across the face!

Angus was quite mortified
His friends were stunned as well
This waitress was demented
Clearly one from Hell
A man at the next table
Having seen her rage unleash
Advised Angus and his friends
'Next time order quiche!'

Mary Wood

My Child

What are you to me, my child
You are the earth, the seas, the world
You are the air in every breath I take
You are the universe unfurled

You are the fire within my heart
The ground on which I race
The wind that blows away my fears
The soft rain upon my face

The birdsong in the morning
The laughter in my ear
The music dancing round my soul
The hands that I hold dear

The moon which sends us rebirth
To start out life anew
A glorious sunrise every morn
Both reminding me of you

This Earth does hold no treasure
For only God can give
The blessing of the sweetest child
That my soul may truly live.

Elizabeth Hale Crompton

On Sitting Outside Windsor Castle After Dropping My Son At The Airport

A castle fortress old in time,
A bastion to defend
Our king or queen in days of old;
And now - a tourist spend!

The glories of an ancient land
Reverberate around.
The thickest walls all tell a tale;
And now - where's history found?

The noise of battle echoes clear,
The sound is loud and low
Of warriors bent on victory
And now - it's just Heathrow!

Carol Hurley

Start Of Day

(Dedicated to the memory of George, my Amstrad word processor)

The wind that scours the sky is from the east,
Here where I sit and glance up from my book
I catch a lightness since my last quick look,
The dawn has reached the Mendips now at least.

And so I rest the book upon my knee
To watch the spreading of the cold thin light,
The windblown spirals of the gulls in flight,
In solitude receive what comes to me.

This is a secret time I do not share,
Before the coming of the crowded day,
When it grows hard for peace to pause and stay,
But I can still remember it was there.

Susan Latimer

Monday Morning Blue

A windswept old bus shelter
Dark skies of rain clouds warning
Stands one lonesome figure
On a grey, cold Monday morning

A middle-aged, ordinary man
Waits and wonders, looking worried
With his ever hopeful dreams
Of the weekend dead and buried

His face is showing the strain
Of that argument with his wife
She's such an insecure woman
But the only one in his life

His expression shows the drain
Of week upon week of stress
And the thought of his daily work
Adds to the mood to depress

His wallet still shows no gain
To aid his problems financial
He's sinking under his debts
Which have become substantial

As well as feeling the pain
Of his very precarious wealth
His burdens are playing a part
In his deteriorating health

The bus comes around the corner
With plenty sad souls adorning
The seats of twenty one
On a grey, cold Monday morning.

Paul Spender

Amy's Rhyme

The cat on the mat.
The rat in the hat.
The hat on the mat.
The mug on the rug.
The bug in the mug.
The bug on the rug.

Amy Cornbill (6)

Maths Made Uneasy

I'm told I have a classic figure worth ten marks out of ten,
But if I gorge myself on pie, what will happen then?
Will my waist just multiply by three point one four two?
Or will my neat circumference, like interest, just accrue!

My pastime is my garden, with lawn a well-mown square,
No logs or ornate tables to spoil symmetry there,
My wife thinks it's too formal . . . a shame she's so obtuse
Because she's such a cute kid when angling for a truce!

Man has tried to square the circle since mathematics first came out,
But all it means to me is a nothing, nil or nowt,
Unless accompanied by a figure with a pound sign in the fore,
On my bank statement (in black of course) well, who could ask
                                                    for more?

History tells us Al Capone was a gangster with a gun,
Not to be compared with Al-Gebra, whose Xs are such fun,
They usually have an equal, which is more than I can say,
About my own 'ex' who divorced me one fine day!

All this is but a fraction of what I *really* want to say,
I calculate without a doubt that this will make your day.
Put two and two together and the answer I might add
Will certainly convince you that I'm well and truly mad!

I feel my number's up at last, Hell beckons me, 'Come in.'
Cos there is no doubt about it, I've led a life of sin,
And when I cross the great divide and Earth is one man less,
My maths teacher will mark my book, 'What a b****y awful mess!'

G K (Bill) Baker

Prince Charming

He came on a snowy white charger, leaving castles in the air,
Leaving behind princesses with diamonds in their hair,
Up the drive he came, not seeing my shabby dress,
Not seeing the curlers in my hair, only a girl in distress.
He smiled and held out his hand
I smiled and lost my heart.
In the moment that his eyes met mine,
I knew we'd never part.

I flew up the stairs, tossing curlers everywhere,
I brushed my teeth and ribboned my hair,
Then I sprayed my perfume on, and wearing my blue sparkly frock
When I floated down the stairs again, his face was full of shock,
In my silver high-heeled sandals,
My hair just reached his chin,
'You smell lovely and look wonderful,'
He said with a mischievous grin.

His shiny armour now was gone, a velvet coat he wore,
And he jumped astride his trusty steed,
And reaching down, so strong indeed,
He swung me up behind him and I snuggled up for more,
And we rode off into the sunset, and that's the way it's been.
A strange and mismatched couple than you have ever seen,
But we laugh a lot and we love a lot,
And I'm glad that he stopped by,
That handsome knight in armour,
With eyes as blue as the sky.

Beryl Partridge

Paradise Lost

Now Mon Repos is very nice,
With pool and yacht and car,
It's opposite to Wuthering Heights,
And next to Shangri La,

It's just across from Bide a While,
It's very near Chez Nous,
And Wee Holme's only yards away,
And so's Dunroamin' too!

Now Mon Repos has everything,
Jacuzzi, sauna, bar,
And all the things you might expect
Next door to Shangri La,

And when I died and went to Hell,
Old Nick said, 'Here you are,'
And gave me such a *lovely* house
- Next door to Shangri La!

Peter Davies

Dreams

We slip beneath the pillow's spell
And drift to where the night wraith dwell,
To lose control of conscious mind
The secrets of our souls to find.
A timeless journey fills our being,
The blind man now becomes all seeing.
The lonely now become the lover,
The childless wife, a loving mother.
Reflection of our dormant fears
Once woken may reduce to tears,
With sleep the master free to prey
On untold thoughts which nightly stray.

Mark L Moulds

Why Couldn't I Be Tall?

I didn't want to be small
Why couldn't I be tall
Like my brothers and sister
Or even my dad?
It's a good job I'm not a lad

I didn't want to be small
Can't even reach the top shelf
And clothes don't fit
Alter them please, oh yes
More than a bit

I didn't want to be small
It's all in your genes
You don't get to choose
It's all worked out
When you're conceived

Oh why couldn't I be tall?

Jacqui Beddow

How Do I Love Thee?

Oh that face!
How I love to watch it change.
The eyes sparkle even before the
shadow box is assessed . . .
. . . the choices are endless.
The lipstick, the gloss!
Alluring, tantalising, smiling.
I am in awe of the magic those hands create
upon that face!
If I could love anything more,
than that vision I adore;
it would be this mirror
which reflects me
to perfection
to be sure.

Vanity Glass

Codger's Holiday

Our chariot? The promenade bench
With coiled cast iron serpent drives
Fresh painted green by Council workers
With yellow teeth and daubed red eyes.

Our journey? Across the wild Welsh bay
The setting sun's red trail below
To distant shores where palm trees sway,
A steel band plays and zephyrs blow.

Our vision? Cool waves lapping toes
Frolicking on the warm white sand
Her grass skirt swinging to and fro,
Strolling, rum and coke in hand.

Our awakening? The hotel supper gong
Echoing through the chilling night
And like two Bisto kids we follow
The rich aroma of Chef's delight.

Our return? Through Victorian splendour
Cast iron jardiniere line the street
Fresh painted blue by Council workers
With silver balls and blackened feet.

John Morgan

Parody On The Last Rose Of Summer

(Based on 'The Last Rose Of Summer' by Thos Moore)

'Tis the last little chocolate, unchosen, alone,
All its lovely companions, devoured and gone.
No ganâche of its kindred, no rose crème is nigh,
To reflect back its lustre and cause sigh for sigh.

I'll not leave thee, thou lone one, to pine in the box,
You'll slip down quite smoothly with 'Scotch on the rocks'.
Thus kindly I bite you, my last luscious gem,
Your mates lie awaiting, go mingle with them!

Gwenyth Eileen Baker

The Letter

Darling Mrs Jones,

I'm in love with you, let's make no bones,
When I saw you at last night's party
Looking oh! so cool and really arty
With flowing tresses and floaty gown.
Lashes beneath eyes of cobalt-blue sweeping down
Onto cheeks of a magnolia hue.
The party-scene faded away and all I saw was you!
I wanted to speak but no words came,
I knew my words would seem so lame.
Like a tongue-tied teenager is how I felt,
Or a knight of old who before you humbly knelt,
I never plucked up courage to speak to you last night,
That is why I am compelled to write
This letter to tell you how I feel.
I know I'm acting like a heel
For you belong to Mr Jones,
Of that let's make no bones.
If there's a chance you feel the same,
Let's not waste time playing silly games.
Let's get together to see if sparks fly,
At least say, we'll give it a try.
If you don't feel so inclined, I promise I'll just let it go.
If you do, you won't regret it, I'll love you forever.

Joe

Ruth Berry

A Glimpse At Life

It looks so inviting that park bench
I think I shall sit there a while
As so many people before me
Have sat, some with a smile
As they looked at life from their viewpoint
Did they wonder, just like me?

How on earth did I reach this park bench?
Life could have gone so many ways
I might have been a priest or prime minister
No less, but seems it was time for delay
As though to teach me a lesson in life
And look at the state of play

As I sit here on the park bench
There are people passing along
Young children with parents bubbling with pride
Birds in the trees throwing their song
Through the air, with apparent ease
And the perfume of blossom never fails to please

I'm glad that I stopped at the park bench
A lady sat by me and said,
'We are bless with a beautiful day my dear.'
I agreed with a smile and a nod of my head
I see wheelchairs too, passing by
With less abled people, who never complain
I have learned to view life with my inward eye
And I'll know, if I pass this way again

Edith Crumb

My Highland Laddie

He promised me a mountain walk,
wild flowers, streams and gentle talk.
I lunged behind, grabbed bracken stalks
like some wrong-footed crow I squawked.
Knee jerking, panting, slid on roots
then heaving, leaping rocks and shoots
fell into hollows, tangled, blocked
collapsed in heather, scratched and knocked.

Our distance widened as he called;
'Come on get up or we'll be caught!'
And sure enough the gusts increased
their shadows merging into mists -
We reached the peak in circling dusk
and settled, soaked on spongy tufts.
'Come on, get up! No time to waste
we must get down; that wind's got tough.'

With slashing rain and rumbling sounds
we stumbled, tumbled, zigzagged down
avoiding tree trunks, boulders, thorns
the heavy sky's encroaching storm.
We pressed on harder, dropped like hawks
squelched through the boglands to the shore
where seal-like stones sloshed back the squalls.
So much for flowers, streams and talk!

Rosemary Keith

The Fly

I'm just a fly, I'm doomed to die,
my life's inconsequential.
It was just as bad for my mum and dad,
to slay them seemed essential.
Whilst I'm the one who must be feared,
the butterfly is much revered.
But I've outmanoeuvred swat and spray
and lived to fight another day.
Another fact I'd like to mention,
the blowfly has a noisy engine,
which makes him easy to locate,
and thus contributes to his fate.
I witnessed what my uncle got,
a victim of a nifty swat,
an inconclusive expiration
yet failed to make resuscitation.
Whilst everyone it seems believes,
that we are all a bunch of thieves.
I love to join you at a meal,
so to survive I've got to steal.
Another hazard I regret,
is the spider with his crafty net.
there are countless dangers to relate,
but I have to fly, as I'm running late . . .

Bill Austin

The Mighty English Oak

I've stood beside this grassy lane, five hundred years or more.
My vigil just to stand and watch and ponder days of yore.
My branches rise up to the sky, my roots are buried deep
Although my trunk is gnarled and stout, my thoughts would
                                        make you weep.
So sit beneath in my cool shade, that I give from my green cloak
And harken thee, give me time, for I'm the mighty English oak.

My brethren once were many, an army on this land.
One hundred thousand, nay, even more, to stand at God's command.
Through snow and hail, rain and shine we stood and gave our seed,
But then came man, a clumsy beast, who just did not take heed.
He plundered as it suited him, for want, for greed, a joke.
He stripped the kingdom clean and bare of this mighty English oak.

He used us to make sailing ships, then gladly went to war
Against his own kind so I hear, oh how the blood did pour.
Then when his ships were lost at sea, he came to us again.
Men stripped us of our mighty boughs and that began the chain
For when the howling rains beat down, into the ground did soak,
Our dying roots were failing, alas, the mighty English oak.

Over many hundred years, the pillage carried on.
So man could make his mark in life, now we are all but gone.
My cousins, ash, the elm, the lime and weeping willow too.
Nought but a memory they will be if left to him and you.
For was it only yesterday, the rook sat here and spoke,
He'd flown for miles to find a perch, on a mighty English oak.

So now it's time, the lane marked out, the trenches they are dug,
The last in line from what was once a massive English wood.
They're coming in at dawn for me, with gangers and machine
To rip my roots out of the ground, to make the landscape clean
Building more nests for greedy men, yes, you and your kinsfolk.
For this is my last evening here as a mighty English oak.

Alan Deane

The Month Of Snow

March 4.05
Snow in layers fall around
Creeps the morning, not a sound!
A strange new whiteness on the ground
A cape upon my roof is found.

The sky hangs low while flakes fall slow
Windows glaze and patterns flow,
A prisoner where I dare not go
Footsteps trapped within the snow.

Brings such beauty to the eye
Small and dainty from the sky,
Dry as wafers watch them fly
Freeze the earth where they now lie.

March brings the coldest yet
Winter months hard to forget,
Spring arrives with a sting
Such treachery this month will bring.

Sally Flood

Old Friends

We dismantle the perennial spruce,
fold its scentless branches in ritual truce,
no needle droppings shower the floor,
just a tuck-away through the attic door.
Faithful garlands, baubles glistening,
an end to eager children listening
to imagined sleighbells on the roof,
tallying every dainty hoof.

With holly leaves and berries withered,
even jovial Santa must have shivered
that myth and magic frosty night,
filling sleepers' stockings in pale starlight.

Old year wrappers again re-sealed
until next yuletide bells are pealed.
You relish the whining Hoover now
since elfin helpers took their bow.
Our home is tidy, clean yet hollow,
time to banish last autumn's sorrow.
Whatever happens to you and me
we'll always love our Christmas tree!

Malcolm Williams

The Way Forward

Had a stroke in 2002
What a battle, what a 'to-do'
Learned to walk again quite soon
But no lazy strolls on a Cumbrian afternoon
Independence lost to me
Now at least, I can make a cup of tea
My partner pushes me in my chair
He even washes and styles my hair
We still go on holidays to Greece
His strength and love never cease
The 'pain barrier' I must often go through
But my poetry I still send to you
Three long years have quickly passed
I can walk with my stick now, ever so fast
My grandchildren help and love me so
And look after me wherever we go
At eight and four, they're only small
But they don't treat me differently, not at all
I often paint and read a lot
And am very thankful for what I've got
I can still see flowers bloom in spring
In the early morning hear birds sing
I long for the sun to bring some heat
And make me more nimble on my feet
But most of all I love my new scooter
It's given me independence
And it even has a hooter!

Jennifer H Fox

More Rubbish

The mail lands with a thud on the mat, here we go again

I don't want a loan
I don't want to change my phone
Are my bills too high?
Is there something I would like to buy?
I don't need a flashy new card
My other one doesn't work that hard
Letters asking if I'm losing my hair
Or do I want to buy this comfy reclining chair?
Do I need my hedges clipped?
Has a disc in my back slipped?
Would I like to sue my neighbour?
Would I like to vote Liberal, Tory or Labour?
Would I like free membership to the latest fitness club?
Do I need safety handles to help me out of the tub?
Do I want insurance for the television or the DVD?
These people can cover me for a modest fee
Do I want to buy the latest copy of the Weightwatcher's guide?
Do I want a mortgage where my money isn't tied?
Do I need a lift to help me up the stairs?
Obviously each one of these people really cares
So into the bin they go without a second thought
If I needed any of these things I would have already bought.

Alan Brafield

To My Surgeon

I am not afraid
When you are there,
No - I am not afraid
Because I'm sure you care.
Where would we be without you?
Truly I do not know -
You carry on your work
Forever on the go.
You bring relief and joy
Every single day,
We all rely on you
As asleep we lay.
You give patients confidence
They feel that they can cope,
Nagging doubts have vanished
Why? You give them *hope*.
You have such a happy face
And a welcome smile
When we awaken it appears
To linger for a while.

Soon I will be home
Feeling really fine,
Accept my grateful thanks
Plus this little rhyme.

Esther Hawkins

Friends

At one o'clock I saw a star
A tiny speck out so far
Just like dust on polished wood
From in a country lane I stood

Much, much later, nearly four
I looked and saw my star once more
Clear and sharp and oh so white
You brightened up the sky at night

And looking again I could see
Many more like you round me
North and south, west and east
A sailor's guide; a stargazer's feast

As the night began to wane
I knew you'd all be back again
And then I hope I shall see
You all shining down on me

Karen Disney

The Last Pit

The giant wheels have now stopped turning
The last man to leave shakes his head,
No more shining black rock coal
This pit is finally finished - dead.

No more crunching of hobnailed boots
Rattling of the iron cast cage,
Vibrant pit has closed his mouth
For a cleaner modern living age.

Taking off their battered headlamps,
Handing over their safety gear
Grimy faces, dirty hands now awash
Mixed with water, soap and tears.

Shovel, spade gone with sweat and toil
Fingers crushed also hearts are too
Will be forgotten with the ending
Of the pit they loved, worked and knew.

Now they leave behind not just a lifetime
But comradeship and loyal friends,
None looking back at the clanging closing gate
The pit - the wheels have stopped - the end.

Jean Neville

Love Sickness

I

The prince, he was a-wailing, he was gnashing hard his jaws,
No matter how he tried to reason still he found no cause
For falling hard and head o'er heels, obsessed he was with Mabel,
Though when he tried to talk to her, his tongue was tied as Babel.
In many languages he wanted to express his pain,
Emotion that he suffered hurts us all, though we'd be fain
To seem like Rupert, serving-man, with cold and gravel heart,
The prince did gravitate towards him, plucked his woeful dart:

II

'Why, oh why, must I deny the sigh that drives a wedge
Between my heart and lovesick mind, no matter how I dredge
The channel deep between them, come I clear with nothing sane
How true it is that madness waits on love, infects the brain . . .'

III

'Oh quiet your nonsense,' said young Rupert, apathy his friend,
'You sound as helpless as a baby, candy to defend,
Just get yourself to Mabel and ingratiate your soul
With hers, her heart, her mind, her body, all her person whole.
Ladies like to hear how lovesick puppies lap their feet,
Get on with you, go find her and don't contemplate retreat.'

IV

Well that was that, the prince dispatched, he tracked young
                                                    Mabel down,
He found her fanning wind away, a solitary frown,
Said, 'Mabel, I now do declare I love you more than life,
To have you as my partner would negate my trouble strife,
Please be mine, young Rupert, he just told me this to say,
And that Lothario is always wont to get his way.'

V

At that did Mabel giggle, laugh, guffaw into his face,
You guessed it, Rupert had already up usurped the place
That rightful love had given to the prince, alas his hope
Its stool was kicked and he left there to hang by rafter my rope.
And so, four letters, an emotion, holds us each in thrall,
More oft than not however it does make fools of one and all.

Chris Griffith

Old Age

We couldn't use the bath, poor souls,
So out the door it went,
To be replaced, a shower we thought,
With every good intent,
But the shower proved more difficult
With the step too high for us,
So out went the shower, no sad goodbye,
And very little fuss.

Then in came all the workmen,
To bring us up to date,
With lovely new shower, and a chair,
On waterproof floor, it's really great.
So now behind the curtain new,
Everything is super,
Just sitting there, with nice hot spray,
And soapy loofar.
To all those 'helping hands' we say,
Our thanks for a wonderful start
To each day . . .

Joan Hammond

Rhyme For Our Time

Cast your eyes around you on the planet where we dwell,
The beauty of the landscape weaves an awe-inspiring spell.
Ponder for a while perhaps, consider what we see -
In amongst the beauty there is squalor lurking free.

Some of this is nature's work, mere Man cannot control,
But much is due to hand of Man in dominating role.
The Lord may send tsunamis that devastate the land,
Hurricanes sweep all before with all-destroying hand.
Avoidance of the dire results is the best way we can cope,
But in this time of nature's force, our God must be our hope.

The culture of the drink and drugs in pub and club now rife
Encompasses the young and old in every walk of life.
The fabric of society, the sense of good and ill
Are rent apart by mindless yobs who mutilate and kill.
In likewise vein the hand of Man reveals capacity
To murder thousands in New York with cold ferocity.

The company of marriage vows seem now so out of date.
Jump into bed, enjoy yourself. The outcome - it can wait!
The bond is weak, the couple break, a family is rent.
All has gone with tragic loss of all that marriage meant.
What breed of man or womanhood can justify the crime
Of murders diabolical, of babies in their prime?

One casts one's eye across the vista of the worldly scene
And sees, alas, the semblance of a dark and nightmare dream.
The picture has a flavour though, it's sad to say it's so,
It reminds one of the fall of Rome in years so long ago.

Tony Channon

Church Island

Tranquil the setting,
At this early hour,
Almost touching the water flow,
A misty morning, lying low,
In the early hours of dawn,
The dew settles on the lawn.
When life has not yet stirred,
And the creatures of the night,
Are in hiding, out of sight;
When the sun does rise,
And the mist clears from the sky,
The island is unique,
The old ruined church,
That is no more,
Left destroyed by nature, wind and rain,
No bell will sound,
Only the birds will sing their song.

Carole Herron

Coving Capers

Decided to put up coving so the ceiling looks straight,
But not being experts we got into a state,
Where did we go wrong? It just will not fit,
The gap's so wide we could fit in a brick.

We read instructions on the mitre cutting block,
Then cut two corners but oh, what a shock,
After two hours of trying and practising a bit,
We finally got the two corners to fit.

Then up with the ladder and on with cement,
We got more on ourselves than we really meant,
Climbed up to the ceiling and carefully we pressed,
We struggled a bit but we did our best.

Next week is more coving, but I know we'll forget,
Just how we cut it, I'll wager a bet,
Perseverance to us is the name of the game,
We'll soon have all ceilings looking the same.

On with emulsion (we're doing it white),
So in the end it will look alright,
Roll over the paper with a colour we've picked,
We are almost there, we have got this licked.

A larger room is next to be done,
But it needs to be 'coved', that's not much fun,
How do those decorators learn this skill?
So the next room we do, I'll call them . . . I will.

Elsie Kemp

Choices

Twenty-first century voices
always offering us
choices . . .

Your head may reel from trying to recall
previous lives you never lived at all
or else - likely to induce a worse state
some which - predestined - are lying in wait
on this overpopulated planet.
Ancestors, posterity, these forget.
Avoid all otherworldly selves floating,
over their life-goals, doting or gloating -
whether overcome by bewilderment
or now joyous, knowing all that is meant.
Such time for revelation is not yet.

How unnerving it is to understand
that from your own thought processes, a strand
may drift off and be lost in time and space
or lodge instead behind another face -
in the mind of a parallel figure
which it may well disrupt - or transfigure . . .

Too much to comprehend one universe,
yet choices you decide not to make
are the very ones your *clones* have to take
through hidden from you in the multiverse.

Twenty-first century voices
always offering us
choices . . .

C M Creedon

Hate

From where does this poison come?
Is it me what have I done?
Hate is a truly massive word.
It is one that should never ever be declared.

It rises up to fill your thoughts.
Keeps you awake as you walk the boards.
From where does it come and in what form?
It is definitely not of the norm.

It begins to fester and take over your every thought.
Once it has you, you are really caught.
It's a fire that takes time to douse.
It's a control that can jail you in your house.

How do we come to really hate?
Because once it starts it is just too late.
How do these thoughts come into your head?
You toss and turn when you are in bed.

Your thoughts all begin to turn nasty and vile.
You want to rest from them just for a while.
Some people enjoy hate, but most do not.
How you are, is just your lot.

It drives some people to even kill.
What type are you, do you fit this bill?
It rips friendships and families so far apart.
It is the number one breaker, of a good person's heart.

It drives you to look deep inside your soul.
At times in reality you are out of control.
I would say it is the Devil's work,
Because your mind is a place where he would lurk.

Tom Roach

Butterfly Wings

Come fly with me on butterfly wings
to my world of make believe,
come listen to the fairies sing
on this magical summer's eve.

Come away with me to a life so new
leave human world for fey.
Come dance upon my morning dew
and watch the break of day.

Come hold my hand, I'll guide you through
you won't believe your eyes.
Come quickly now, I'm begging you
before the moon does rise.

Come to me, step through my world
feel the power of the rainbow's hue.
Come fly with me, let wings uncurl
fairy love for you is true.

Come fly with me on butterfly wing
I know you'd come to me.
Anoint yourself with fey blessing
my world I give to thee.

Karen Canning

The Ant

I tried to befriend an ant today,
He turned up his antennae and walked away;
'Am I not good enough for you?' I cried!
Then I realised his friend had died.
He carried his body, it looked kind of flat.
I wondered for a moment how he'd got like that,
Then it dawned, it could have been me.

They do risk their lives! (The ants I mean)
Wandering all over their parochial domain;
With all kinds of hazards along the way.
Human feet are large! A thousand
Times bigger than the ant, perhaps more!
Of this I am not a hundred percent sure.
Although, I won't bother with the research,
I'll just be more careful where I tread and I lurch.

The able-bodied ant continued his task,
He found a crevasse in the slabs at last.
I would not be surprised if there's a lab down there,
As part of their subterranean lair,
Where flattened ants are brought back to life;
Because they are oh so clever!
Though, maybe not singular, but as a whole.

John L Wigley

Untitled

What do you think you are doing to me?
I know you'd like me to open wide,
So you can peer in and see.
All this equipment makes so much noise.
Only you play around with them
As if they were toys.
'Open up wide, I'm entering now.
I'll take it easy, this I know how.
Just a small prick,
You won't feel any pain.
There for a while,
You'll have to remain.
I'm just going to start prodding and poking some more,
It's too late to make a dash for the door.
So close your eyes, I'll do the rest.
I've been given good references,
Been told I'm the best.
Just turn your head a little this way,
You'll feel a lot better,
At the end of the day.'
Now it's all over,
I'm out the door.
I couldn't have laid there,
Taken any more.
I'm never going back to that place again.
Cos the dentist was rough,
And caused so much pain.

Anne-Marie Richardson

It's Legal, So That's All Right Then!

From the year nineteen-ninety, in civilised UK,
Let simple death statistics have their say.
Cannabis - zero, ecstasy - 3, but,
Thirty thousand 'boozers' in eternity.

Who comes out top with the highest score?
Not smack at sixty-two, or methadone at eighty-four.
Guess who wins the 'kick-the-bucket' bet?
At one hundred and ten thousand, it's 'Mr Cigarette'.

The politician says he understands,
But industry has tied his hands.
Let's demonise drugs, but drink? Come off it,
Forget the principle - look at the profit.

We need this tax, such welcome wealth,
Covers the cost of our poor health.
And being British we'd surely miss,
The blackouts, the fights, the vomit, the risk.

Danny D Morris

Seashell Sanctuary

Defiant dendrites fissure refracted delight
From swirling seconds encapsulated pink and white
Resurrecting a recalcitrant existentialistic gloom
The all-pervasive phantom's scintillating plume

Somnambulant shadows of paranoia coalesce
Long-subjugated sentinels of reason acquiesce
Vertiginous visions metamorphose and die
The chemical quisling's insubstantial alibi

Frayed fragments of reality remain
Sparse scaffolding within a schismatic brain
'Retreat, Retreat' the call tolls like a bell
To pseudo-sanctuary in a cranial seashell.

Julian F Murfitt

A Clip Round The Ear

Nobody doubts it, the facts are all there
It's reported in graphic description
Crime today is worse, so very much worse
Than it was in the days of conscription

But why should the forces take in the debris
They've enough to do, that is quite clear
No, the answer to this is not rocket science
All it needs is a clip round the ear

Discipline-free days are all well and good
In fairy-tale land, that is true
But in these times of reality and crime
Do-gooders just don't have a clue

In learning the difference between right and wrong
What's so bad about old-fashioned fear
Of teachers, policemen and yes, mums and dads
All it needs is a clip round the ear

The vandals and bullies would surely think twice
Before causing such trouble and angst
If they only knew that if they got found out
They'd be punished with no further chance

Of course, everyone wants to feel safer
Two thousand and five's full of fear
If only MPs would be brave and decree
All it needs is a clip round the ear

Shirley McIntyre

Anchor Books Information

We hope you have enjoyed reading this book - and that you will continue to enjoy it in the coming years.

If you like reading and writing poetry drop us a line, or give us a call, and we'll send you a free information pack.

Alternatively if you would like to order further copies of this book or any of our other titles, then please give us a call or log onto our website at www.forwardpress.co.uk

Anchor Books Information
Remus House
Coltsfoot Drive
Peterborough
PE2 9JX

(01733) 898102